# Introduction

The 'traditional' tale is a story that has been told again and again by tellers whose skill in performance has ensured its survival. The process is continuous, plots and protagonists being constantly repeated: some with social connotations (stepmothers, landless younger sons) and some magical (the numbers three and seven, fairies and witches and ghosts). Animals assume human attributes, as in the story of the hare and the tortoise, or they prove to be changelings, as in stories of selkies, worms, or frog princes. What is certain is that, whether they are part of our collective unconscious or the result of centuries of emigration during which they travelled with their storytellers, traditional tales are ancient and worldwide.

In printed form, therefore, the traditional tale is really a script for a storyteller speaking, performing, *acting* the story. Transmitted from generation to generation by word of mouth, the tales were first written down by collectors for the purpose of preservation and scholarly study. Gradually, as literacy has become universal, the traditional forms of oral storytelling have survived only as a minority art form and as a diversion for children.

Historically, traditional tales were not just toys for children. They belonged to the whole community, as the chief source of entertainment. When children became a separate group in society, and belief in the supernatural fell into disrepute among rational adults, traditional tales were left to the young and their carers, and to the illiterate.

Now attitudes are changing again. I am not alone, I think, in believing that traditional tales deserve the widest possible audience, and that their appeal is not confined to narrow age limits. Let the tales find their listeners where they may. For that reason the title of this bookguide is *Traditional Tales* and not *Traditional Tales for Children*. I am aware, however, that the readership of a Signal Bookguide consists of adults interested in sharing literature with children, so all the books included have been selected because they contain stories – or more accurately, versions of stories – which young people should encounter. Most of the books have been published as children's books, and their presentation, format, and illustrations reflect this. All of them repay the attention of the individual reader, but all gain from being read aloud so that they can be shared by a group. The large anthologies in particular benefit from having an adult act as selector and storyteller.

I started telling traditional tales when meeting every week a dozen school classes of multilingual children visiting the library where I had just taken up my first professional post. I was stumbling towards the idea that stories from around the world, not necessarily from the countries of origin of the children, would be a common bond between us. I noticed that they were good, exciting stories and that children enjoyed them.

Years later, when I began reviewing folk and fairy tales regularly, I became fully conscious of their central importance in children's fictional experience. Out of the mass of ephemeral material, traditional tales shone with immediacy, musical prose, a sense of shared experience. As an enthusiastic reader of fantasy, I was also reminded that traditional tales are endlessly plundered for plots and characters, so it would be profitable and wise to explore these sources. I am convinced that, with the limited time available for reading, and the limited attention and enthusiasm of some children, it is vital to offer them fiction in the undiluted richness of its traditional form.

The arrangement of the guide divides the tales into categories that indicate some aspects of their role in modern literature.

*Fables* (entries 1 to 13) considers the antiquity of the beast fable, and its survival into modern times.

*Legends and Hero Tales* (entries 14 to 34) looks at the mythical characters whose fictional reputations have grown over the centuries.

*Traditional Tales from around the World* (entries 35 to 78) is the largest section but covers only a fraction of the relevant material. Examples of story groups have been chosen for their intrinsic worth as well as for their geographic origin.

*Traditional Fairy Tales* (entries 79 to 99) brings us to the work of the best-known translators of tales to the page, the French Perrault and the German Brothers Grimm.

*Literary Fairy Tales* (entries 100 to 113) recommends modern stories written to traditional patterns.

*Traditional Tales for the Under-Sixes* (entries 114 to 127) recommends editions for young children.

*Collectors and Retellers* (entries 128 to 139) recommends standard works that provide secure guidance for anyone new to sharing traditional tales with young people.

*Source Books* (entries 140 to 145) lists some background reading for adults.

Brers Wolf and Rabbit telling tales on the porch
in *The Tales of Uncle Remus: The Adventures of Brer Rabbit*
by Julius Lester, illustrated by Jerry Pinkney
(Bodley Head) entry 10

In compiling the guide, I met some problems with terminology. 'Traditional tale' seemed the most helpful over-all term. 'Folk tale' and 'fairy tale' have been used interchangeably by editors, though 'fairy tale' in the title generally indicates that the book is intended for children. 'Legend' is usually agreed to mean a story grown from a seed of historical fact. 'Myth' is defined by Kevin Crossley-Holland as ' . . . a dramatic narrative through which humans try to explain to themselves their origins on this planet and the wonders they see around them. . . . sacred history set in a mythical time.' (*The Norse Myths*, page xxxix)

What to call the audience was also a problem. Since the stories are made for hearing, 'listener' would seem more appropriate than 'reader' – but both activities are possible and to be encouraged. I have normally preferred 'reader' as the term which implies all activity contributing to the reading process, including listening and talking. 'Child' was not acceptable, for the reason already given –

that the stories properly belong to all, to adults as well as children.

Problems about availability became clear during my initial trawl of titles. Users of this bookguide are bound to notice favourites missing because they are out of print. But it is worth remembering that a school library service should be able to offer a wide selection of traditional tales, including out-of-print titles.

After much hesitation, I decided to include a suggested age range for each book as an indication of potential readership. You are invited to ignore this in favour of your own pressing reasons for wanting to tell a story. The place you and any children with whom you are sharing stories have reached in your exploration of fiction is far more important. The ages given suggest the times when children may tackle the books as readers. Being able to listen to a story read or told extends the age range, and the opportunity of letting teenagers rediscover basic story forms should always be considered.

Finally, this is a bookguide, not a booklist. Each volume has been chosen as a representative of its kind as well as for its particular worth. I hope that readers will be encouraged to use the guide as a basis for exploration as well as a means of discovering recommendable versions of the tales to which they feel personally attached.

Thanks are due to the librarians of Gloucestershire County Library, Arts and Museums Service, who have worked on the county's folk- and fairy-tale exhibition 'The Enchanted Castle' since 1985, and to teachers and pupils who have seen the exhibition. Many of the ideas in this bookguide have come from them.           MARY STEELE

The symbol □ indicates titles in a picture-book format.

# Fables

Said to be among the oldest surviving stories are the fables told by a Greek slave, Aesop, who lived about the year 600 B.C. Some of the stories attributed to him may be even older in origin, for they have been found in India and China, where they were being told long before Aesop was born. The tradition of Aesop's storytelling continued long after his death, with newly invented fables being added to the collection right up to the time of La Fontaine.

Teaching a lesson is the special characteristic of a fable from

Aesop. Sometimes this is implicit in the story, sometimes it is expressed in a separate 'moral'. The other characteristic that distinguishes the fable from the folk or fairy tale is the predominance of animal characters. J.R.R. Tolkien has defined such tales as 'stories in which the animals are the heroes and heroines, and men and women, if they appear, are mere adjuncts; and above all, those in which the animal form is only a mask upon a human face, a device of the satirist or the preacher . . . ' (*Tree and Leaf*, page 20).

We know very little about Aesop, but the stories that bear his name teach many of the simple lessons of everyday human behaviour ('Pride comes before a fall', 'Slow and steady wins the race', 'Sour grapes') and this is what makes them so particularly appealing to children of primary school age, who can match the antics of the animals with their own experience.

The fables are short and to the point. They are amenable, therefore, to constant anthologizing, adaptation and illustration. Quite a few versions are worth having ready at hand: some modern retellers spell out the moral at the end of each story, others prefer to leave it to be deduced by the reader.

☐ 1. The Donkey and The Dog, twenty fables *retold by Joan Tate, illustrated by Svend Otto S.*
[0 7207 1722 1, Pelham, £5.95. Ages 5 to 11.]
Joan Tate's style encourages us to reflect on what we are being told. She does not spell out the morals. Watercolour paintings on each page face the story and give individuality to the characters.

☐ 2. Foxy Fables *retold and illustrated by Tony Ross*
[0 86264 126 8, Andersen, £5.95; Picture Puffin, £1.95. Ages 6 to 10.]
The six fables in this book feature a typical crew of animals, but Tony Ross has drawn them against the background of a big city, and has made details of the stories fit this environment. For example, Fox lures Goat into a drain instead of a well, and Hare and Tortoise challenge each other to a race during a row in a wine bar.

3. Once in a Wood *retold and illustrated by Eve Rice*
[0 00 672090 0, Fontana Young Lions, £1.75. Ages 6 to 9.]
Eve Rice retells ten fables in rhythmic, non-rhyming verses, harmonizing text and black-and-white illustrations effortlessly into the I Can Read format suitable for six-to-nines.

[7]

☐ 4. One Fine Day in Summer *retold by Max Bolliger,*
*translated by Sarah Gibson, illustrated by Jindra Čapek*
[0 86264 228 0, Andersen, £6.95. Ages 7 to 11.]
Six fables within one fable make an intriguing framework for these
tales from Aesop. Fox, raven, tortoise, peacock, crow, wolf and
dog all meet and tell fables with each other as the protagonists. Each
animal is embarrassed by the story told against himself, and the
ensuing fight is heard by the lion, shown as a magnificent biblical
specimen. To make peace he tells the story of how he was saved by
a mouse. The book is interesting both in conception and in design.
As the animals quarrel, they are shown crossing the page away from
their companions.

There are many picture-book versions of single fables. Among
some of the best –

☐ 5. The Hare and the Tortoise *retold by Caroline Castle,*
*illustrated by Peter Weevers*
[0 330 29179 3, Piccolo, £1.99. Ages 5 to 11.]
The well-known fable is elaborated on in text and illustrations. The
animals are given the human trappings of clothes and houses in
illustrations of detailed jokiness.

☐ 6. The Lion and the Rat *version by La Fontaine,*
*illustrated by Brian Wildsmith*
[0 19 279607 0, Oxford U. P., £5.50. Ages 3 to 7.]
The most striking aspect of the book is the representation in
glowing colour of the animal characters. A simple text points the
moral so that the story is clear and satisfying for a very young child.

☐ 7. The Miller, his Son and their Donkey
*illustrated by Eugen Sopko*
[0 200 72920 9, Abelard/North-South paperback, £2.95. Ages 5 to
9.]
The setting is a sultry summer landscape where the few strangers
encountered by the protagonists all feel within their rights to
interfere. The foolish miller and his son blindly follow every
conflicting piece of advice, and our sympathies end with the
donkey. As well as sunny illustrations, this version features well-
spaced, large clear type for early readers.

☐ 8. The Goose That Laid the Golden Egg
*retold and illustrated by Geoffrey Patterson*
[0 233 97878 X, Deutsch, £5.95. Ages 5 to 9.]
A fable against greed, given a farmyard setting and illustrations made with chalk on brown paper, which intrigue young children.

☐ 9. The Tale of Johnny Town-Mouse
*written and illustrated by Beatrix Potter*
[0 723 23472 8, Warne, £3.50. Ages 6 to 9.]
The fable of the town and country mouse is one of Aesop's most frequently adapted stories, expressing the human need for roots and routine. Beatrix Potter, dedicating the book to 'Aesop in the shadows', retells and illustrates it with her characteristically precise and detailed observation and the quietly expressed feeling of a writer for whom country holidays had been happy interludes in a restricted town girlhood.

All down the years traditional tales, as well as offering entertainment, seem to have acted as a means of communication for the oppressed. Aesop, a slave, could not overtly comment on his masters' behaviour, but he could poke fun at their human frailty through his animal fables. In the same way, the black slaves of the southern states of the USA told stories of Brer Rabbit, which were first recorded by a white journalist, Joel Chandler Harris, using an invented character, Uncle Remus, as the storyteller. In recent years this framework has become socially unacceptable, and now a new version of the stories has been published.

10. The Tales of Uncle Remus: The Adventures of Brer Rabbit *by Julius Lester, illustrated by Jerry Pinkney*
[0 370 31089 6, Bodley Head, £9.95. Ages 6 to adult.]
Julius Lester retells the stories without Uncle Remus, using his own voice instead. Another factor inhibiting the use of these tales was the dialect in which Harris couched them, rendering them difficult even for professional storytellers. Lester has removed the dialect and written in a simpler, modified form of contemporary black-American English, which frees the tales for us to enjoy. The Brer Rabbit tales are satirical, often very funny, and sometimes brutally frank about human foibles.

The most famous of newly invented beast fables are the tales by Rudyard Kipling, which he wrote for his 'Best Beloved' – the 'Just

So Stories' that can surely turn any reader-aloud into a natural storyteller.

11. Just So Stories *written and illustrated by Rudyard Kipling*
[0 333 08793 3, Macmillan, £7.95. Ages 6 to 12.]
In *Just So Stories* Kipling added to the satisfying explanations of the origins of creatures the panache of his own idiosyncratic style. Originally Kipling illustrated his stories with all the unexpectedness he brought to his writing. The complete Quarto Edition includes these illustrations.

The expiry of copyright in Kipling's work in 1987 brought a rash of new editions. His own publisher, Macmillan (on behalf of the National Trust), got in first with a series of single-story volumes illustrated by different hands (Charles Keeping, Quentin Blake, William Stobbs among them) with varying degrees of success. Together, they make an appealing and colourful approach to the stories that attracts some less willing modern young readers in a way that perhaps the one-volume collections do not.

Michael Foreman has illustrated *Just So Stories* for Viking Kestrel and Puffin Classics (£7.95 and £1.95). And recently Methuen began a series of newly illustrated individual stories in small, compact format. In *How the Whale Got His Throat* Jonathan Langley complements Kipling's idiosyncratic style and captures the comedy of the story. Also available: *How the Camel Got His Hump* and *How the Rhinoceros Got His Skin* (Methuen, £2.95 each).

12. How the Whale Became *by Ted Hughes,*
*illustrated by George Adamson*
[0 14 030482 7, Young Puffin, £1.99. Ages 6 to 12.]
'Now God had a little back garden' is a first sentence guaranteed to still a child audience with surprise; this is not the usual introduction to God's activities. Ted Hughes has constructed clever, teasing hypotheses for the evolution of the animals. In the Young Puffin version the book has been unfortunate in the choice of illustrator; the cover is garish.

13. Tales of the Early World *by Ted Hughes,*
*illustrated by Andrew Davidson*
[0 571 15126 4, Faber, £5.95. Ages 8 to adult.]
Twenty-five years after *How The Whale Became* was published (1963), Hughes has come back to the same setting in a book of new stories. While *How the Whale Became* is written in a relaxed, conversational style that recommends it to young children, the later

From 'The Trunk'
in *Tales of the Early World*

volume is made out of tough language, chiselled into shape. Sometimes the tales are dramatic, sometimes philosophical, occasionally acid. The cover is black, covered with staring eyes. A book for older children and teenagers.

## Legends and Hero Tales

Whereas the fable, like the parable, tells a story in which we can very often recognize ourselves in the animal characters, hero tales and legends are peopled with supermen whose exploits inspire marvel and wonder. Such tales were often told in the early Christian centuries by the harper or poet, who was a person of some importance in the community. The opening lines of our greatest English poem, *Beowulf*, set the scene:

> In the hall of the king of the Geats, a hundred men listened. Almost silence. The cat-fire hissed and spat, golden-eyed tapestries winked out of the gloom. Silence. The man rose from the stranger's seat.
> 'Your name?' demanded Hygelac.
> 'Gangleri,' said the stranger. 'In your tongue: Wanderer.'
> 'All right, Wanderer. It's time you sang for your supper.'
> Men on the mead-benches shifted their buttocks, and stretched out their legs. The gathering faced inwards towards the fire.
> Wanderer stood in the poet's place by the hearth and rubbed his one gleaming eye. 'I'll fuel you,' he said, 'with a true story,

[11]

and one close to my heart. This story of past and present and future . . .'

. . . Wanderer stooped and scooped up six-stringer, the harp that always stood in the poet's place. Gleaming maplewood, white willow pegs, white fingertips, a quivering face.

'Listen!' said Wanderer. 'A story of heroes!' Now he plucked the harp with a plectrum. 'A story of monsters!' And plucked it again. 'A story of Denmark!'

□ 14. Beowulf *translated by Kevin Crossley-Holland, illustrated by Charles Keeping*
[0 19 279770 0, Oxford U. P., £5.95; paperback, £2.50. Ages 10 to adult.]
This translation (quoted above), poetic and insistently rhythmic, reproduces the epic nature of the struggle between the hero and the monsters Grendel, the she-hag, and the dragon who is Beowulf's doom. Children from around ten through secondary school can be drawn into the ferocious grandeur of this dramatic story, graphically expressed by Charles Keeping's black and white illustrations.

15. Dragon Slayer *by Rosemary Sutcliff, illustrated by Charles Keeping*
[0 14 030254 9, Puffin, £1.75. Ages 9 to adult.]
Rosemary Sutcliff's treatment of the Beowulf poem expands the

text to the length of a short novel, and describes the events in a dignified prose. *Dragon Slayer* has been recorded as a two-cassette audio set (read by Sean Barrett; Chivers Children's Audio Book, CCA3014, £9.25). It is a well spoken, effective performance, apart from the intrusive announcement of the start of each new chapter.

Charles Keeping illustrated both retellings of *Beowulf*, and it is interesting to compare his response to different texts, with a gap of twenty years between them.

NORSE MYTHS

16. Northern Lights: Legends, Sagas and Folk-tales
*edited by Kevin Crossley-Holland, illustrated by Alan Howard*
[0 571 14809 3, Faber, £4.99 paperbound. Ages 11 to adult.]
A distillation from previously published Faber books of *Northern Legends* and *Northern Folktales*. Stories from Grimm and the British Isles mix with selections from the Scandinavian tradition and extracts from sagas and lesser known hero tales. A concise, approachable introduction to works from the historic northern literature.

'This is an evil story that you tell, my friend.'
A Charles Keeping illustration from *Dragon Slayer*

## 17. Axe-Age, Wolf-Age
*retold by Kevin Crossley-Holland, illustrated by Hannah Firmin*
[0 233 97688 4, Deutsch, £7.95; Faber, £4.95 paperbound. Ages 13 to adult.]
A condensed edition of a magnum opus, Crossley-Holland's translation of the Norse myths. The myths are retold in a dramatic and exciting style, which matches the violent and supernatural events being described. This great story cycle begins with the creation of the Frost Giants and the establishment of the gods in Asgard, and ends with a vision of Ragnarok – the end of the world. The myths describe the constant enmity between the gods and the giants, a war often waged through magical trickery, so that there is a grim humour in some of the stories. In 'Thor's Expedition to Utgard' the god of thunder, famous for his strength, is unable to empty a drinking horn or defeat an old crone in a wrestling match, when he is challenged by a giant. After his humiliation he is told that the end of the horn is in the sea and that the old crone is old age, whom nobody can defeat. A streak of cruelty runs through the myths, exemplified in Loki, the trickster god, who steals Idun's apples, which the gods must eat to stay young, and is father to three hideous monsters. His evil nature drives him to cause the death of the wise and gentle god Balder; for this crime he is bound in eternal torment. *Axe-Age, Wolf-Age* is an intense and demanding work, and merits a complete and attentive reading to gain an understanding of the tangled web of relationships and extraordinary physical prowess combined with the gods' dangerous naivety.

## 18. Myths of the Norsemen *retold by Roger Lancelyn Green, illustrated by Brian Wildsmith*
[0 14 035098 5, Puffin, £2.25. Ages 9 to 14.]
Lancelyn Green aimed for a fluent narrative, written in a solemn and dignified style, reflecting the different qualities of the stories, from poetic to burlesque, always overshadowed by tragedy, which reaches its climax in the death of Balder.

IRISH MYTHS

## 19. The High Deeds of Finn Mac Cool *by Rosemary Sutcliff, illustrated by Michael Charlton*
[0 14 030380 4, Puffin, £2.50. Ages 10 to adult.]
Finn MacCool (his name is variously spelt) is a hero from pre-Christian Ireland and parts of Scotland. He is the leader of the

Fianna, the warrior band who guarded the green south of Ireland. The legends deal with the constant raiding and the defence of the kingdom against invasion. The Fianna are proud, loyal and argumentative, laid under bonds to accept any challenge, even those imposed upon them by the magic whose thread runs through the stories. The account of great deeds is tempered with romantic interludes such as the love of Finn for enchanted Saba. Rosemary Sutcliff weaves the stories together into a continuous narrative. She leaves the reader with a sense of loss for the passing of heroic days, and a feeling of the sorrow that must come to Finn.

20. Finn Mac Cool and the Small Men of Deeds *retold by Pat O'Shea, illustrated by Stephen Lavis*
[0 19 274134 9, Oxford U. P., £5.95. Ages 8 to 12.]
The predominant tone of Rosemary Sutcliff's book is that of hardness and grandeur with some lightening in the story of the Giolla Dacker's horse, which runs away with fourteen of the Fianna. There is a more boisterously humorous side to the Finn tales and this, together with the magic, is brought out in Pat O'Shea's entertaining short book. Finn is set under a spell to protect a king's baby from a great hand which has snatched two previous children up the chimney. He leaves the Fianna behind him, and his helpers for the task are a crew of seven with impossible skills (able to hear anything, climb anywhere, support any weight), which he will employ one by one as the story progresses. The cheery, fantastical tale is complemented by Stephen Lavis's comic-strip line drawings and decorations.

21. Fionn Mac Cumhail, Champion of Ireland
*retold by John Matthews, illustrated by James Field*
[1 85314 001 5, Firebird Books, £4.95 paperbound. Ages 12 up.]
The background of the legend of Finn is less well known than that of the Arthurian stories, with which they can be compared. In a series called 'Heroes and Warriors' John Matthews describes the historical, military and archaeological evidence for the world of the Fianna and retells eight of the stories.

WELSH LEGENDS

22. Tales from the Mabinogion *retold by Gwyn Thomas and Kevin Crossley-Holland, illustrated by Margaret Jones*
[0 575 04343 1, Gollancz (Lynx paperback), £5.95. Ages 11 up.]
The Mabinogion is a collection of eleven magnificent Welsh tales,

preserved in manuscripts which date from the fourteenth century. The major group of stories within the collection, the Four Branches of the Mabinogi, are retold here. In them the exploits of the hero, Pryderi, are interwoven with other tales, making a complicated narrative with many episodes. Perhaps the best-known incident (thanks to Alan Garner's novel, *The Owl Service*) is the story of Blodeuwedd, a woman magically made out of flowers, who is turned into an owl as a punishment for betraying her husband. *Tales from the Mabinogion* presents to young people an enthralling and demanding work of literature. The extraordinary events described in the text are portrayed in black and white drawings and full-page, full-colour paintings.

23. The Quest for Olwen *retold by Gwyn Thomas and Kevin Crossley-Holland, illustrated by Margaret Jones*
[0 7188 2706 6, Lutterworth, £8.95. Ages 11 to adult.]
Another tale from the Mabinogion and a companion volume to entry 22. It is a richly imagined, vastly entertaining stew of a story whose ingredients include a young prince, a curse, a giant, a series of impossible tasks and King Arthur. This lavishly illustrated book divides the tale into chapters, which help us cope with the piling on of events, and treats the notorious long lists of weird characters with considerable humour, the retellers acting as editor and commentator. The complex narrative (and the small type in which it is set) may discourage readers at first, but the story repays all the demands it makes.

24. Welsh Legends and Folk-tales *retold by Gwyn Jones, illustrated by Joan Kiddell-Monroe*
[0 14 031097 5, Puffin, £2.95. Ages 10 to adult.]
If the excitement and drama of *The Quest for Olwen* has given you an appetite for the ancient Welsh tales, this compilation can be turned to, offering as it does the four branches of the Mabinogi, plus stories of the Welsh Arthur and Welsh folk tales. The majority are not well known. There is a legend of Arthur sleeping under a hill, tales of changelings taken by the Fairies, and the sorrowful tale of the fairy woman from the lake of Llyn-y-Fan, who returned under water, taking everything she had brought with her, after being struck three 'causeless blows' by her husband. One popular story is included here, the tale of the hound who was unjustly slain after protecting his master's baby from a wolf, but the hound's name, Gelert, by which the story is best known, is not used.

25. The Sword and the Circle; The Light Beyond the Forest; The Road to Camlann *each written by Rosemary Sutcliff, illustrated by Shirley Felts*
[0 340 28562 1, 0 340 25821 7, 0 340 32100 8, Knight, £2.50, £1.95, £2.50. Ages 10 to adult.]
The legends of King Arthur have been told, written and sung innumerable times. Stories making up the Arthurian tradition appear in ancient Celtic tales, Germanic hero stories and French chivalric lays. The historical Arthur has been exhaustively discussed, and archaeological sites have been romantically attributed to him (Cadbury/Camelot, for example). Unlike Finn MacCool, another Celtic hero, our image of Arthur is indelibly marked by three writers: Malory in the fifteenth century, Tennyson in the nineteenth, and T.H. White in the twentieth.

Out of this richly embroidered tapestry, Rosemary Sutcliff has rewoven the stories with exceptional clarity. She acknowledges her great predecessors and also touches on other sources. Her version, in three volumes, is tender, reflective and strong. She draws sympathetic portraits of the doomed Tristan, jealous Geraint, bad-tempered Kay, and magical Gawain, and overcomes the difficulties of treating Arthur's incestuous son Mordred and the relationship with Lancelot, Guenever and the King. A simple image, that of the whitethroat calling, connects the moment of Arthur's conception with the grievous parting of the lovers Lancelot and Guenever.

The stories of Arthur have been widely represented in the visual arts over the centuries, and the romantic images of the Victorian revival still loom large. Two recent picture books offer contrasting styles of illustration:

☐ 26. Sir Gawain and the Loathly Lady *retold by Selina Hastings, illustrated by Juan Wijngaard*
[0 7445 0295 0, Walker, £6.95; paperback, £2.50. Ages 9 to 13.]
☐ 27. The Lady of Shalott *by Alfred, Lord Tennyson, illustrated by Charles Keeping*
[0 19 276057 2, Oxford U. P., £4.95; paperback, £2.95. Ages 10 up.]
Juan Wijngaard, in his Greenaway prize-winning illustrations to *Sir Gawain and the Loathly Lady* and, less successfully, *Sir Gawain and the Green Knight*, returns to the Middle Ages and the jewel-like art of the manuscripts. Charles Keeping contrasts the classic poem – a

pleasure to read aloud if you do not let the verse structure take over completely – with stark black and white pictures of a four-square castle, exhausted workers, an armoured knight on a heavy horse and a bleak woman slumped in a chair.

Another interesting point about these two books is the treatment of women in the Arthurian legends. Female characters are, by and large, doomed to be passive victims or sirens. By a confusion of stories that seem to mock the victims further, the death on the barge of the Lady of Shalott is also enacted by Elaine, who tricks Lancelot into bed, bears his son, Percival, and then is rejected by him. An unusually assertive heroine, however, is Linnet, who goads and bullies Beaumains, the kitchen knight in *The Sword and the Circle* (entry 25), and there is the loathly lady, who expresses woman's greatest desire: to have her own way. This could be a clarion call to liberation or the utmost male patronage, depending on how you interpret it. In order to speak so frankly, the woman has to be hideously ugly, disguised, bewitched. Rosemary Sutcliff adds a sad coda which works the episode into the rest of the cycle – something a picture-book treatment of an isolated episode cannot do – developing Gawain's character and hinting at the sombre tragedy to come.

and something of Gawain went with her. He was a valiant knight still, but his old blazing temper returned upon him and he was less steadfast of purpose and less kind than he had been; and he went hollow of heart for her sake, all the remaining days of his life.

Title-page drawing from *Proud Knight, Fair Lady*

[18]

☐ 28. Proud Knight, Fair Lady *translated by Naomi Lewis, illustrated by Angela Barrett*
[0 09 173511 4, Hutchinson, £10.95. Ages 10 to adult.]
The twelve Breton lays of Marie de France were collected and written down by her in the twelfth century. They are all love stories, sharing a world of medieval chivalry with Arthurian romance. The tale of Lanval is set at Arthur's court, and the lays include a brief, poignant episode in the love affair of Tristan and Iseult. 'Bisclavret' is the story of a werewolf; children who are attracted by the 'horror' aspect of the tale are left moved by the dignified sorrow of the spellbound hero. Here is a rare opportunity to share these exquisite lays with young people. The tone is measured and the language heightened, but any distance this may create for the contemporary reader is bridged by the powerful depiction of characters imprisoned by jealousy and trapped by love. Angela Barrett's painted borders and initial letters and full-page pictures achieve a dramatic intensity and emotion absolutely in tune with the long-ago author's voice.

ROBIN HOOD

Robin Hood and King Arthur are probably the two most popular and oft-quoted heroes of British legend. Their attractions are very different. Robin, though raised to the earldom of Huntingdon in some versions, is famed as a rebel outlaw and thief, cocking a snook at legitimate, even if corrupt, authority, quite unlike King Arthur, who stands for high-minded honour, justice and courtly chivalry. Robin's companions are erstwhile shepherds, artisans and peasants, plus a renegade friar, and the setting is the historical Middle Ages, though the exact reign varies. In contrast Arthur and his knights exist with magic in a dream landscape.

Newer than the Arthurian legends, the tales of Robin are first mentioned in print in 'Piers Plowman' in 1377 but were circulated by minstrels for some time before that. Since then he has turned up in May Games, chapbooks, opera, numerous retellings, on screen and as the straight lead in the pantomime *Babes in the Wood*. Historians have chewed over whether he ever really existed, and tourist boards have seized upon the slightest hint that he, or one of his companions, set foot upon ground they wish to advertise. A couple of mentions in Shakespeare are the nearest Robin gets to a great writer. He benefited from no Malory or Tennyson but has flourished in the rough and tumble of popular culture as perhaps befits a hero of the common man.

29. Robin Hood and the Men of the Greenwood *by Henry Gilbert, illustrated by Walter Crane*
[0 946495 62 9, Bracken Books, £4.99. Ages 9 to adult.]
A moment of celebration in my frequently depressing trawl through *British Books in Print* (so many wonderful books no longer there) came when I discovered that the Henry Gilbert version is still in print. At the same time I reread the article by Philippa Pearce in *Children's Literature in Education* (Vol. 16, No. 3), in which she describes the impact of this book upon her as a child and the 'dazzling' pictures of Walter Crane. Pearce points out that Robin is wholly heroic, powerful and mysterious, connected by Gilbert with the legend of the Little People. The Ian Serraillier ballads of Robin in the Greenwood which, read aloud, gave exactly the right rhythm to the stories, are sadly out of print.

30. The Adventures of Robin Hood *by Roger Lancelyn Green, illustrated by Arthur Hall*
[0 14 035034 9, Puffin, £2.50. Ages 9 to 13.]
An accessible, inviting read combining an immediacy for children with a solid grounding in the history of Robin Hood literature, extracts from which Roger Lancelyn Green uses as chapter headings, thus easily bridging the gap between past and present for the reader. This Robin is the famous swashbuckling hero and sweetheart of Maid Marion (who did not exist in the earliest stories, but is usually included in modern versions).

Librarians, teachers and parents will be aware of the demand for Robin Hood stories from young children. Julian Atterton contributes two short novels, *Robin Hood and the Miller's Son* and *Robin Hood and Little John* (the more successful), to the Redwing series (Julia MacRae, £3.95 each), targeted at seven-to-elevens. Ruth Manning-Sanders gives us a simple picture-storybook version also called *Robin Hood and Little John*, illustrated by Jo Chesterman (Methuen, £4.95; ages 6 to 9).

This is a convenient point to discuss the place of TV tie-ins and game books as transmitters of traditional tales. Robin's translation onto celluloid, most recently in *Robin of Sherwood*, seems to be an entirely appropriate development in his fictional life. TV and film can be used to open up the dialogue with children about the preservation and passing on of stories. Apart from the tie-in books, other editions of Robin Hood stories benefit too, at least to the extent of a new jacket in which Robin is portrayed with a resemblance to the TV actor playing the role. I am less sure about the game books: the chances of abrupt death are too high, and hardly fit in with the legendary ability to survive. They also lack any story pattern. However, game books have plundered epic and legendary stories for their plots, and teachers and librarians have reported that some game-book devotees are encouraged to explore the sources further. The *Robin of Sherwood* stories and game books are available from Puffin.

□ 31. William Tell *retold by Nina Bawden,*
*illustrated by Pascale Allamand*
[0 224 01940 6, Cape, £4.95. Ages 6 to 9.]
William Tell (another recent presence on children's television) is a hero best known now for the overture named after him (and usurped as a signature tune by another hero, the Lone Ranger). Nina Bawden writes a simple outline of the story about the splitting of the apple and Pascale Allamand provides bright, colourful pictures.

Felicity Trotman has written about William Tell for the Methuen 'Great Tales from Long Ago' series, an unexceptional set of brief encounters with heroes of legend and myth, which are convenient introductions for children and useful as reading for older 'reluctant' readers. The series includes Greek legends (Midas, Odysseus, Theseus and the Trojan horse), King Arthur, and the folk-tale exploits of Dick Whittington, the Pied Piper and Rip van Winkle. Available in hard and paperback picture-story format.

GREEK LEGENDS

32. The Faber Book of Greek Legends *edited by Kathleen Lines,*
*illustrated by Faith Jaques*
[0 571 13920 5, Faber, £5.95 paperbound. Ages 9 to 14.]
The myths of ancient Greece are studied as literature by a minority these days. They are most likely to be encountered in primary school projects or as part of a secondary school myths and legends theme. There is an urgent need for books that can convey the power of the stories while assuming no previous knowledge on the part of the reader. Some years ago Kathleen Lines offered herself as a wise and experienced guide in *The Faber Book of Greek Legends*. This has recently been reprinted. Lines chooses extracts from nineteenth- and twentieth-century sources, covering tales of the gods, their rivalries and encounters with humans, and leading up to the events

and aftermath of the Trojan War. There is an index and a bibliography, which, while many of the books are out of print, provides sensible criteria for selection.

33. Tales of the Greek Heroes *retold by Roger Lancelyn Green, illustrated by Betty Middleton-Sandford*
[0 14 030119 4, Puffin, £2.25. Ages 9 to 14.]
Along with Lancelyn Green's *The Tale of Troy* (Puffin, £1.95), retellings of the legends and tales of Ancient Greece 'as the Greeks themselves thought of them, as the history of the Heroic Age'. Starting with the Coming of the Immortals, the books include the Story of Prometheus, the Labours of Heracles, the Adventures of Theseus, the Quest of the Golden Fleece, the Battle with the Giants, the Siege of Troy, and the return of Odysseus and the other Heroes to Greece. The use of dialogue and colourful dramatic description gives the writing pace and variety.

34. The Legend of Odysseus *compiled and illustrated by Peter Connolly*
[0 19 917065 7, Oxford U. P., £7.95; paperback, £3.95. Ages 11 to adult.]
Peter Connolly concentrates on the portrayal of the ancient world, alternating extracts from the Odyssey with factual material about the history of Bronze Age Greece and pictorial reconstructions based on art and archaeology. This linking of myth with historical evidence is regretted by Elizabeth Cook in her standard-setting book, *The Ordinary and the Fabulous* (entry 142), but is a popular activity both in schools and in TV documentaries. This book cannot prove legendary heroes to be historical figures, but it does enrich our understanding of the context in which the stories were first told.

# Traditional Tales from around the World

Traditional tales have, of course, always travelled with their creators and tellers, and have taken root wherever there are people who will tell them. The patterns of traditional tales exist everywhere and regularly recur in stories found in every culture and every language. Whenever – and wherever – traditional tales are collected and written down, changes must take place in the translation from an oral source to a written text. Different collectors have treated this problem in different ways. In our own time, and in our own British Isles, both Alan Garner and Kevin Crossley-Holland have demonstrated the ways in which the life of the spoken word can be re-created on the printed page.

35. Book of British Fairy Tales *retold by Alan Garner,*
*illustrated by Derek Collard*
[0 00 184048 7. Collins, £4.95 paperbound. Ages 9 to adult.]
Alan Garner's approach to the traditional tale is to reproduce the spoken voice, not by phonetic spelling, but by attempting to capture the rhythms of dialect speech and the phrasing and diction of a particular region. *British Fairy Tales* is a core collection for me, and for anyone who wishes to become attuned to Britain's heritage of traditional tales. The stories are told with unparalleled vigour and drama.

'Tom-Tit-Tot' is the witty Suffolk equivalent of the Grimms' story 'Rumpelstiltskin', which is always extremely popular with children. 'Mally Whuppy' is a rough and tough version in which royalty does not appear (compare the picture-book version by Errol Le Cain, entry 44) but the heroine comes from sturdy farming stock not dainty about admitting a killing.

> Mally Whuppy plucked a hair out of her head and made a bridge of it, and she ran over the river, and the giant could not cross.
> 'You are over there, Mally Whuppy,' said the giant.
> 'I am, though it is hard for thee.'
> 'You killed my three bald brown daughters.'
> 'I killed, though it is hard for thee . . . .'
> 'When will you come again?'
> 'I shall come when my business brings me.'

'The Paddo' is a brief and charming variant of 'The Frog Prince'. 'Mr Fox' is the equally brief but chilling Bluebeard story collected by Joseph Jacobs, in which the atmosphere is built up with the refrain 'Be bold, be bold', until we hear 'Be bold, be bold, but not too bold,/ Lest that your heart's blood should run cold.' A particular pleasure to tell is 'Kate Crackernuts', a story of adventure and romance.

All these are proof, if proof were needed, that traditional tales are not for small children only. Try any of them with teenagers and

[23]

they will be absorbed and demand more. Secondary school pupils love being read aloud to, and traditional tales such as these have all the power to hold them, just as they held their original adult audiences in times past.

'But it's queer stitching altogether that's been going on here . . .'
from *A Bag of Moonshine*

36.   A Bag of Moonshine *by Alan Garner,*
*illustrated by Patrick James Lynch*
[0 00 184403 2, Collins, £8.95; paperbound, £4.95. Ages 7 to 12.]
The most recent and light-hearted of Garner's collections concentrates on the fools, gowks and nonsense-makers of folk tale. The book's vigour is softened with gentler stories like the one about the fate of proud 'Alice of the Lea'.

Both *British Fairy Tales* and *A Bag of Moonshine* benefit from excellent illustrations, giving the stories a dignified frame in the first, and depicting the colourful characters in the second.

[24]

37. Folk-Tales of the British Isles *edited by Kevin Crossley-Holland, illustrated by Hannah Firmin*
[0 571 13786 5, Faber, £9.95. Ages 13 to adult.]
In this brilliant survey of the field, the tales are arranged thematically under twelve headings such as 'Fairies', 'Origins and Causes', 'Fabulous Beasts', 'Ghosts' and 'Saints and Devils'. Each section is introduced by a discussion of the theme and some notes on the individual tales. Victorian curiosities, reminiscences, ballads and jokes are mixed with histories in dialect and uncommon versions of well-known traditional tales. The stories are chosen by an editor who has a poet's ear for the music of language.

*British Folk Tales* (Orchard, o.p.) is similar in title but different in concept. These are new versions, with Crossley-Holland's authorial voice rephrasing the traditional material. The emphasis is on individual characterization, often developed through dialogue. The single volume went swiftly out of print, but small illustrated books reprinting groups of the stories have now been produced, ideal for putting into a child's hand. (*Boo!; Dathera Dad; Small-Tooth Dog; Piper and Pooka*, Orchard, £3.95 each).

38. English Fairy Tales *collected by Joseph Jacobs, illustrated by Margery Gill*
[0 370 01023 X, Bodley Head, £4.95 paperbound. Ages 13 to adult.]
Joseph Jacobs was one of the scholarly folklorists of the late nineteenth century. When he began to assemble a collection of English fairy tales, English stories were considered 'all but lost' by his fellow scholars. He opened his preface to the first edition (1890) triumphantly: 'Who says that English folk have no fairy tales of their own?' (Incidentally, he ignored the northern boundary so that he could include lowland Scottish stories.) Jacobs's achievement was to collect eighty-seven English traditional tales and record them in a form meant to be read aloud. The combined advantages of scholarship, accessibility and an intended audience of children have made his work into a valuable source book frequently plundered by the compilers of anthologies and by illustrators hunting for a suitable text to turn into a picture book.

The most popular nursery tales are here, as, for example, 'The Three Little Pigs', and the great haunting tales: 'Childe Rowland', 'The Laidly Worm of Spindlestone Heugh', 'The Black Bull of Norroway' and 'Tamlane'.

The Bodley Head edition, reprinted in paperback, includes both original volumes, *English Fairy Tales* and *More English Fairy Tales*, as well as Jacobs's prefaces, notes and references. These are worth reading for his description of his method of work, and his suggestion that the stories were nearly lost in the chasm that divides the English classes. He also touches on the vexed question of what to call traditional tales. He chose fairy tales because that was the name used by children in the 1880s. *English Fairy Tales* is available in a Dover paperback facsimile of the first edition, with plentiful illustrations by John D. Batten; *More English Fairy Tales* is no longer in print with Dover.

39. English Fables and Fairy Stories *retold by James Reeves, illustrated by Joan Kiddell-Monroe*
[0 19 274137 3, Oxford U.P. (Myths and Legends Series), £3.95 paperbound. Ages 8 to 12]
James Reeves has retold nineteen English fairy tales, expanding on the stories set down by Jacobs by giving names to the characters and fleshing out details of the situations and background. His relaxed, conversational treatment of the stories occasionally blurs the traditional patterns but makes them pleasant, inviting and approachable for teller and audience.

Chapter-head drawing for 'Jack and the Beanstalk'
in *English Fables and Fairy Stories*

40. Strong Tom *by Maggie Pearson, illustrated by Larry Wilkes*
[0 340 42580 6, Hodder & Stoughton (Rooster), £3.95. Ages 6 to 9.]

'Under any circumstances no English child's library of folk-tales can be considered complete that does not present a version of Mr Hickathrift's exploits.' Thus Joseph Jacobs in his note to the abridgement given in *English Fairy Tales*. Maggie Pearson has arranged the story to suit a series for six-to-nines, and succeeds in harmonizing the requirements of the format with the pattern of the episodes and conversational rhythm of the story, which tells of Tom's superhuman strength employed against a tree, a giant, a rival for his girl's hand, and finally (comic echoes of *Beowulf*) a dragon. A cheerfully relaxed introduction to English traditional tales.

Just a few picture-book versions of English folk tales. Others are recommended in the section 'for under-sixes' (entries 114 to 127).

☐ 41. King of the Cats *retold and illustrated by Paul Galdone*
[0 437 42531 2, World's Work, £4.50. Ages 6 to 12.]

☐ 42. A Strange Visitor *retold by Mary O'Toole,*
*illustrated by Craig Smith*
[ 0 333 48711 7, Macmillan (Kookaburra), £1.75. Ages 6 to 10.]

☐ 43. Jack and the Beanstalk *retold and illustrated by Tony Ross*
[0 14 033118 2, Puffin, £1.95. Ages 6 to 11.]

☐ 44. Molly Whuppie *retold by Walter de la Mare,*
*illustrated by Errol Le Cain*
[0 571 11942 5, Faber, £5.95. Ages 6 to 11.]

☐ 45. The Three Wishes *retold and illustrated by Paul Galdone*
[0 437 42500 2, World's Work, £5.50. Ages 6 to 9.]

*King of the Cats* makes an ideal tale to round off a storytelling session, or to use when a short snatch of narrative is called for. Paul Galdone's illustrations add humour and a visual focus in their depiction of the huge black cats with staring yellow eyes, walking upright towards the terrified gravedigger.

In Mary O'Toole's cumulative tale the strange visitor to an old woman manifests itself by instalments from the feet up. The story is ideal for group performance as children will soon join in the repetitions and the final shout 'FOR YOU!' when the visitor reveals what he has come for. Craig Smith shows a cosy woman in dressing gown and fluffy slippers whose armchair is gradually filled by an enormous skeleton.

Tony Ross's comical pictures in *Jack and the Beanstalk*, milking the plot for all it's worth, attract older children and get them looking closely at picture books. The pages are packed with sharply observed details.

Errol Le Cain's illustrations for *Molly Whuppie* add decorative and lively detail to the story, which is given in slightly shortened form. *The Three Wishes* has parallels in Greek myth. The man with the sausage attached to his nose, after he has made two foolish wishes, is an irresistible scene for illustration, and the tale is short, which is an advantage when used as a picture-book text.

☐ 46. Chicken Little *retold and illustrated by Steven Kellogg*
[0 09 171610 1, Hutchinson, £5.95; Beaver, £2.50. Ages 6 to 9.]
Some tales are so well known that illustrators feel confident in playing with the plots to suit their own styles. 'Chicken Little', otherwise known as 'Henny Penny', is not a favourite of mine, so I cheerfully welcome Steven Kellogg's elaboration of the story, which includes a chase by police helicopter piloted by a hippo (hippolice – that kind of humour). Young children may love the unadulterated story with its repetition and funny names. It is included in *The Fairy Tale Treasury* (entry 138) and *The Three Bears & 15 Other Stories* (entry 115).

47. The Broonie, Silkies and Fairies *by Duncan Williamson, illustrated by Alan Herriot*
[0 86241 087 8, Canongate, £7.95; paper, £3.95. Ages 8 to adult.]
Duncan Williamson is a Scottish traveller and a distinguished story-teller among his own people. Since 1980 he has been settled and his stories have been taped and transcribed. Thus the process of preserving traditional tales continues to the present day. This example of his work is particularly rich in the dreamy sad stories of the sealwife (the silkie), trapped into marriage with a human who has stolen her sealskin until she is able to find her animal coat and return to the sea, leaving husband and children behind to mourn.

48. The Well at the World's End *by Norah and William Montgomerie, illustrated by Norah Montgomerie*
[0 86241 093 2, Canongate Kelpie, £1.80. Ages 8 to adult.]
These thirty-five folk tales from Scotland are notable for the exuberance of the narrative. The pace is lively, and most of the stories briefly told – three or four pages in the paperback edition. There is a glossary, but dialect has been anglicized for ease of reading. Some stories are translated from the Gaelic and half a dozen

Illustration for 'Saltie the Silkie'
in *The Broonie, Silkies and Fairies*

have versions in *English Fairy Tales*, though the Montgomeries' title story is called 'The Three Heads in the Well' in Jacobs, for whom 'The Well at the World's End' is 'The Frog Prince'. So closely are traditional tales interbred and then renamed. The book includes two stories of Finn MacCool, which were collected in Argyllshire, including 'Finn MacCool and the Small Men of Deeds' (see entry 20).

**49.** Ghosts and Bogles *by Dinah Starkey, illustrated by Jan Pieńkowski* [0 434 96440 9, Heinemann, £7.95; paperback, £3.95. Ages 8 to 13.]
Sixteen British traditional tales, based on the antics of supernatural creatures. Whuppity Stoorie is a female Tom-Tit-Tot, the moon is captured by will-o'-the-wisps, and there are good and bad ghosts, one of whom is laid by the Dauntless Girl, who is not afraid of anything, however unnatural. Each page of the vigorous, pacy retellings is framed by a different illustrative border.

☐ **50.** Colm of the Islands *retold by Rosemary Harris, illustrated by Pauline Baynes*
[0 7445 0700 6, Walker, £8.95. Ages 8 to 13.]
A Scottish romance, in which kindness to animals is rewarded by their assistance. When Colm's ladylove is captured by the sea king, Colm's animal friends help him to rescue her and release Colm from a spell which detains him in the sea king's palace. The fairly long text is organized successfully into the picture-book format with each spread consisting of a full-page illustration and a small vignette at the head of the text, which is enclosed in a frame. Without being unduly fey Pauline Baynes creates the colourful, weird under-water kingdom in which Colm and his lady are held captive.

AFRICA

The Anansi stories originated in the West African Ashanti kingdom, a wealthy nation with a gold currency. Anansi is the Ashanti word for spider. Usually he is a sly and cunning trickster, a lazy character except when making mischief. He is represented either as a spider or as a man-spider. Whether animal or man, he is at the centre of events, and a picture of a whole society builds up around him in the stories. When the Ashanti were taken naked into slavery across the Atlantic they brought their stories with them to the West Indies and mainland America. The following books trace that journey.

☐ 51. A Story, A Story *retold and illustrated by Gail E. Haley*
[0 410 75190 3, Methuen, £5.50. Ages 6 to 11.]
A marvellous book for introducing the idea of the shared heritage
of story to audiences of any age. The Ashanti people say that it is
Anansi who is responsible for all the stories in the world. He
brought them from Nyame the sky god, who kept them in a box
under his golden stool. How Anansi paid the price is the subject of
this picture book, in which Anansi is represented as a wise old man
who spins a web to the sky.

An animated film treatment of the book is available with a
soundtrack of music played on African instruments. Filmed picture
books, available for hire or purchase, and sometimes from library
services, are a helpful resource for use with large audiences and are
a good way of sparking off discussions with secondary school
students about different methods of telling a story, book design
compared with animation, the use of sound effects and music. *A
Story, A Story* and other videos of traditional tales are available from
Weston Woods, 14 Friday Street, Henley on Thames, Oxfordshire
RG9 1AH.

52. Tales of an Ashanti Father *by Peggy Appiah,
illustrated by Mora Dickson*
[0 233 98126 8, Deutsch, £4.50 paperbound. Ages 7 to 12.]
Peggy Appiah is a white English woman who married a Ghanaian.
Bridging the two cultures, she is an excellent interpreter of the tales
of Kwaku Ananse, originally told in the Asante language, which has
no written form. Peggy Appiah has adapted them in a prose that is
pleasant to read, discreetly including information about the setting
of the stories without interrupting the narrative. Anansi stars in
most of the stories. Others describe the attributes of animals or
explore the origins of social customs.

☐ 53. Oh Kojo! How Could You! *by Verna Aardema,
illustrated by Marc Brown*
[0 241 11375 X, Hamish Hamilton, £7.95; Picturemac, £2.50. Ages
5 to 10.]
Anansi is here duping the gullible Kojo in a story which, for its first
half, shares a plot with 'Jack and the Beanstalk'. 'It isn't one thing,
it isn't two things. It's Anansi,' cries Kojo's long-suffering mother
as the boy sells their possessions for a dog, a cat and a dove. The
dove proves to be the Queen Mother of the Doves and rewards
Kojo with a magic wealth-bringing ring. This leads to a second

part, in which Anansi steals the ring, and the dog and the cat set off to retrieve it. When the dog refuses to carry the cat across the river, the cat completes the quest without him, and is rewarded with privileges for the race of cats forever denied to dogs.

Verna Aardema has sought to translate a storytelling voice onto the page, using the mother's cry as a chorus, and including the sounds of movement and the noises of the river, 'Pon-pon-pon-PON-sa!' The illustrations are full of energetic larger-than-life characters in a colourfully drawn setting.

□ 54. Mufaro's Beautiful Daughters
*retold and illustrated by John Steptoe*
[0 241 12228 7, Hamish Hamilton, £7.95. Ages 8 to 13.]
This spellbinding romantic tale from Zimbabwe has the plot structure of a journey during which various tests are undertaken (see also *Mother Holle*, entry 89). The tests are failed by the proud sister Manyara and overcome by the good sister Nyasha, who marries the snake-king. Reading this picture book was a rediscovery for me, as I told the story many years ago to classes of junior school children under the title 'The Snake with Five Heads'. The illustrations are superb, glowing paintings.

African animal stories are brightly illustrated and simply retold by Mwenye Hadithi and Adrienne Kennaway in a series of picture books: *Crafty Chameleon* (which won the 1987 Kate Greenaway award), *Greedy Zebra, Hot Hippo*, and *Tricky Tortoise* (each Hodder & Stoughton, £6.95; Knight paperback, £2.50; ages 3 to 7). *Hot Hippo* has been published as a 'Big Book', one of a number of scrapbook-sized soft-cover books originated in Australia. They are intended for children with special needs for whom the giant type of the Big Book may alleviate visual impairment or grab the attention of those who are easily distracted. They are also ideal for use with large audiences. (Hodder & Stoughton, £9.95)

□ 55. The Wishing Tree *retold by Usha Bahl,*
*illustrated by Heather Dickinson*
[0 233 98206 X, Deutsch (Storytellers), £3.50. Ages 5 to 9.]
Available in English, Vietnamese, Bengali, Gujarati, Urdu and Hindi. Bilingual picture books retelling traditional tales emphasize the internationalism of folk tales, apart from their other obvious benefits in a multicultural society. 'The Wishing Tree' is an African animal story I used to tell to classes of children of whom a high

proportion used English as a second language. The story hangs on the ability of an animal to remember the word which unlocks a spell on a tree so that it provides food in a drought. After a series of grander animals have tripped over anthills or slid down mountains, the tortoise succeeds in remembering the word correctly, as do the listening children helped by the repetitions.

The history of Anansi stories continues in:

THE AMERICAN HERITAGE FROM AFRICA

56. West Indian Folk-Tales *retold by Philip Sherlock,*
*illustrated by Joan Kiddell-Monroe*
[0 19 274127 6, Oxford U.P. (Myths and Legends Series), £2.95 paperbound. Ages 13 to adult.]
Launched in the 1960s, the Oxford Myths and Legends series provided readable scholarly collections of tales from around the world. This book of West Indian stories traces their journey from the Arawak and Carib peoples of South America to the shores of the Caribbean islands, through the trauma of slavery and the forced immigration of West African peoples. Man begins as a companion to the animal characters, but the stories tell of a gradual separation into hostility. The tale which describes how men and animals stopped talking to each other tells of a great flood such as appears in other mythologies, including the one in the Old Testament.

It will repay the storyteller, when selecting stories from this collection, to read the whole book first in order to become familiar with the context of each tale. *West Indian Folk-Tales* is a valuable source book for secondary school children and adults.

57. Listen to this Story: Tales from the West Indies
*retold by Grace Hallworth, illustrated by Dennis Ranston*
[0 416 58270 2, Magnet, £1.99. Ages 6 up.]
An inviting title, and the welcome is there throughout this book of 'Nanci stories from Trinidad. Grace Hallworth has written them down from her childhood memories, and they are suitable to share with quite a young audience. An acknowledged storyteller in her own right, Grace Hallworth has included a story, 'The Kiskadee', that she invented to explain why the bird of that name cries 'Qu'est-ce que qu'il dit?' The illustrator represents Anansi as an eight-limbed man, who features in the majority of the tales.

# 7. Papa Bois

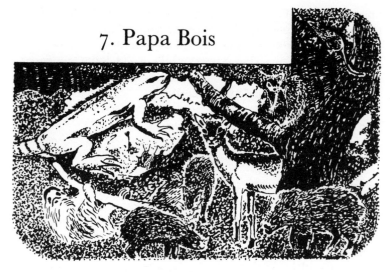

From *Mouth Open, Story Jump Out*

58. Anancy-Spiderman *by James Berry, illustrated by Joseph Olubo*
[0 7445 0793 6, Walker, £7.95. Ages 9 to 14.]
For older readers James Berry, a noted poet and short-story writer, has produced a book of Anansi stories (Anancy is the Jamaican spelling). His style of writing demands close and careful reading or listening to appreciate fully the pattern of his language. He writes in the present tense, using a mixture of dialogue, verse, repetition of words and short sentences to drive the story along. 'Wind works whipping up Blazing-Fire, making Blazing-Fire increase in leaps and spread. And Blazing-Fire smokes bad-bad like a great pile of burning and moves quick-quick towards Anancy's doorway.'

59. Mouth Open, Story Jump Out *retold by Grace Hallworth, illustrated by Art Derry*
[0 416 23550 6, Methuen, £6.95; Magnet, £1.75. Ages 9 to 14.]
Seeking to re-create the casually informal storytelling parties of her West Indian home, when tales of the supernatural would be conjured from the landscape and her people's history, Grace Hallworth links the stories by grouping them in subjects, beginning each group with an introduction and then letting the stories flow in a relaxed way from one to another within each chapter. A book as enjoyable for children to read for themselves as it is to read aloud to them.

60. The People Could Fly: American Black Folktales *retold by Virginia Hamilton, illustrated by Leo and Diane Dillon*
[0 7445 0524 0, Walker, £12.95. Ages 12 to adult.]
Black slaves in the United States were stripped of their languages and racial heritage but they could not be deprived of their collective imagination, fed by what they remembered of their old world. This book is an awe-inspiring tribute on a big scale to Virginia Hamilton's quality as a writer, and to the spirit of the slave story-makers. In her introduction, Virginia Hamilton points out that the tales were a mocking reflection of plantation life. Brer Rabbit is smaller and weaker than the other animals, but he outwits them by his cunning. Later on, a slave character, usually called John, assumes the trickster role in tall stories and gruesome yarns. There are supernatural tales, dreams of freedom, and celebrations of actual escapes. The story featured in the title and on the cover is an astonishing fantasy in which the slaves re-enact their ancient ability to fly away home. With full-page and half-page illustrations by an award-winning pair of artists, this book is outstanding in every way.

NORTH AMERICAN INDIAN TALES

An acquaintance with Amer-Indian folklore is an important correc-tive to the dancing-round-bonfires simplification of Hollywood stereotyping. Only a tiny remnant is left of the lifestyle of the tales, but the stories revive shadowy pictures of many different peoples spread across a continent.

61. The Faber Book of North American Legends
*retold by Virginia Haviland, illustrated by Ann Strugnell*
[0 571 11038 X, Faber, £4.99. Ages 10 to adult.]
Virginia Haviland studied folklore for many years, and out of her experience and access to sources (she was in charge of the children's section of the Library of Congress, Washington, D.C.) she com-piled this valuable source book that makes a good introduction to American traditional tales. As well as Indian and Eskimo tales, she includes tall tales, some stories of the black Americans, and tales brought by immigrants from Europe.

Entries 62 to 65 are picture-book versions of Amer-Indian tales.

☐ 62. Blue-Jay and Robin *retold and illustrated by Joanna Troughton*
[0 216 91375 6, Blackie, £5.95. Ages 6 to 9.]
Blue-Jay is a trickster, who visits his animal friends, is fed by magic, teases his friends in return, and is finally reconciled to them with a great feast. The simple repetitive structure uses the refrain 'Magic is not for you, Blue-Jay'. The illustrations, filling each doublespread to the edges, introduce us to the animals and environment of the forest-dwelling Chinook Indians. Joanna Troughton has illustrated other Amer-Indian stories. *How Rabbit Stole the Fire* (Blackie, £6.50) comes from the woodlands in which Rabbit robs the Sky People of the secret Fire. As he passes it on from animal to animal, the fire burns distinguishing physical marks which the animals have to this day. Saucy Rabbit bounces through the pictures. *Who Will Be the Sun?* (Blackie, £6.95) is another creation story involving the Coyote the Trickster story of the Plains Indians. Blazing heat and brilliant animal masks dominate the pictures.

☐ 63. The Girl Who Loved Wild Horses
*retold and illustrated by Paul Goble*
[0 333 32176 6, Picturemac, £2.50. Ages 8 to 13.]
Amer-Indian tales have attracted artists of high quality, among them Paul Goble, who chooses stories which urge an understanding of the Indian way of thinking and the forces dictating their life. This one is romantic and spirited, describing a girl who preferred to live with the horses than with the people of the tribe, and eventually became one of the creatures she worshipped. The tale shows the Indians' strong affinity with the animals they tame. Two songs about the mystery of horses are included.

The way of life of the Plains Indians depended upon the existence of huge herds of buffalo. This is the source of *Buffalo Woman* (Macmillan, £5.95), a Comanche and Blackfeet story, in which a brave marries a buffalo who has taken human shape. Another of Paul Goble's books, *The Great Race of the Birds and Animals* (Collins, £5.95), takes the the story of the buffalo hunts on the plains and emphasizes the communion of men and animals, and the responsibility of being human. All Goble's books are supported by brilliantly coloured pictures, scholarly notes and references.

☐ 64. The Legend of the Bluebonnet
*retold and illustrated by Tomie dePaola*
[0 416 45340 6, Methuen, £5.95. Ages 6 to 9.]
A gentle, solemn story about the flower which is now the state

[36]

emblem of Texas. The theme is far-reaching and topical: a drought and famine have been caused by Man's selfishness. In this story the subject is approached in a way that young children can sympathize with. A young girl makes a childlike but, to her, great sacrifice to save her people. Tomie dePaola's characteristic bold outlines and simple backgrounds are used effectively to show the starkness of the setting and the patient dignity of the long lines of Comanche, waiting for the rain.

☐ 65. The Star Maiden *retold by Barbara Juster Esbensen, illustrated by Helen K. Davie*
[0 316 24951 3, Little, Brown, £6.95. Ages 7 to 10.]
A lyrical creation story from the Ojibway people about stars coming to earth as water lilies. Romantically told and delicately illustrated with borders based on Ojibway patterns, it is a contrast to the stories of survival in a harsh landscape depicted by Goble and dePaola.

Look out for a strange tale linking the fall of Napoleon with an Amer-Indian charm, retold in *Folktales and Fables of the World* (entry 78).

RUSSIA

66. Old Peter's Russian Tales *retold by Arthur Ransome, illustrated by Faith Jaques*
[0 224 02959 2, Cape, £6.95. Ages 7 to 11.]
As a young man, Ransome was studying folklore in Russia just before the revolution. In retelling the stories he collected, he invented the kindly old Peter as the narrator and the small grandchildren Vanya and Maroosia as the audience. It is a sentimental device, and the cheerful description of Russian peasant life paints a rosy picture which can hardly have been true for the majority of real peasants at that time. However, it allows Ransome to link, with a neat introduction and satisfying ending, stories which are strong and exciting – classic folk tales that have kept the book deservedly in print seventy years after its first publication. 'The Firebird' is there, as is 'Baba Yaga', the witch with the iron teeth, and 'The Fool of the World', whose ship is crewed by men with extraordinary powers.
  *The War of the Birds and the Beasts* (Cape, £5.95; ages 11 to adult), a collection of darker stories for older children, was assembled by

Hugh Brogan from manuscripts prepared by Ransome, but never published owing to the combined pressures of war and revolution in 1917. In his interesting introduction, Brogan explains how Ransome would translate several variants of a story and then make a good composite version in English. Stories include the touching 'Swan Princess', the cautionary 'Costly Ring', in which three brothers marry for gain and then lose the fortune quarrelling, and a number of tales about God, death and saints.

James Riordan reveals an equally rich, powerfully sombre vein of stories in his *Russian Gypsy Tales* (Canongate, £7.95; ages 11 to adult).

67. Ivan: Stories of Old Russia *retold by Marcus Crouch, illustrated by Bob Dewar*
[0 19 274135 7, Oxford U. P., £7.95. Ages 8 to 12.]
A comic counterpoint to the romanticism of *Old Peter* and the harshness of *Russian Gypsy Tales*, these light-hearted stories are about the Russian equivalent of our Jack: foolish Ivan (who gets everything wrong and is beaten for his pains) but also fortunate, cheerful Ivan. The tales are retold in an easy conversational tone, and Ivan's antics, shown in colour on every page of this large-format book, will encourage even unenthusiastic readers to browse.

ASIA

68. Folktales from Asia for Children Everywhere, Book 3 *compiled by Yunesuko Ajia Bunka Senta, illustrated by various artists*
[0 8348 1034 4, Phaidon, £4.95. Ages 7 to 11.]
Six volumes (Books 1 and 2 are out of print; 3 to 6, £4.95 each) published under the Asian co-publication programme with a policy of stories being selected, retold and illustrated by writers and artists of the countries of origin. Countries represented are India, Pakistan, Nepal, Japan, the Philippines, Malaysia, Burma, Iran, Korea, Afghanistan, Indonesia, Thailand, Singapore, Sri Lanka, Vietnam, Cambodia and Laos. A compilation from numerous Asian nations edited by a committee sounds appallingly cumbersome, but the result is a valuable and charming miscellany.

In Book 3, for example, 'The Carpenter's Son', from Afghanistan, is similar to *Oh Kojo! How Could You!* (entry 53). The same volume gives the Vietnamese explanation of the Man in the Moon, as well as an Indonesian story which concludes with a race, not between hare and tortoise but between mouse-deer and snail, and a Lear-like tale (without the tragedy) about a youngest daughter who is disowned by her father for refusing, unlike her sisters, to say that he rather than God provides the food. Her fortunes are restored with the aid of a fairy who, somewhat unnervingly, bleeds with rubies when her head is chopped off.

From *Seasons of Splendour*

69. Seasons of Splendour *by Madhur Jaffrey,*
*illustrated by Michael Foreman*
[0 907516 58 0, Pavilion/Michael Joseph, £8.95; Puffin, £5.95. Ages 9 to 12.]
Madhur Jaffrey, of TV cookery fame, links her choice of folk tales and stories from Indian mythology with an account of her affluent childhood, which sets the stories in an interesting context and creates a bond between author and reader. The whole book has a feeling of richness about it, appropriate to its title. The large format, the full-page pictures in colour and line, the leisurely conversational style of the telling make a book ideal for dipping into and returning to many times.

*The Indian Storybook* by Rani Singh (Heinemann, £6.95; paperback, £3.95) retells similar stories with simplicity and clarity, and its format recommends it to young readers.

70. The Stupid Tiger and Other Tales
*by Upendrakishore Raychaudhuri, translated by William Radice,*
*illustrated by William Rushton*
[0 233 98201 9, Deutsch, £2.95 paperbound. Ages 9 to 12.]
A selection and translation from a classic book of Bengali folk tales

written during the nineteenth century in the traditional style. Once again, the characters are animals. The stories are action-packed adventures, during which wickedness and stupidity are ruthlessly exposed and punished. Not for the squeamish but great for those who like plenty going on in their fiction.

Two Indian traditional tales in picture-book editions:

☐ 71. The Wizard Punchkin *illustrated by Joanna Troughton*
[0 216 92376 X, Blackie, £6.95. Ages 6 to 10.]
This fairy tale of a kidnapped princess, a handsome prince, and a wicked wizard whose soul lies in an egg is illustrated in a pastiche of Indian styles.

☐ 72. The Moon Hare *retold by Susheila Stone,*
*illustrated by Heather Dickinson*
[0 233 98208 6, Deutsch (Storytellers), £3.50. Ages 5 to 9.]
Available in English and as a bilingual picture book in Bengali, Hindi, Punjabi, Urdu and Chinese. A gentle fable from India in which the duty of feeding the poor is preached. The hare, having nothing else to give, offers itself to a beggar. The beggar is the god Sakka, who rewards the hare by painting his face on the moon. The text is superimposed on line and wash illustrations.

73. The Spring of Butterflies *translated by He Liyi,*
*illustrated by Pan Aiqing and Li Zhao*
[0 00 184137 8, Collins, £7.95. Ages 10 to 14.]
Stories set in China have appeared in collections, but the cultural revolution in that country prevented any interchange with the West for many years. He Liyi preserved stories of China's minority peoples and translated them into English under conditions of great difficulty. The tales, whose plots deal with courage and victory, and self-sacrifice in the face of natural disasters, are extremely powerful. Storytellers are revered in China and a sharing of their tradition is to be eagerly anticipated.

☐ 74. The Willow Pattern Story *by Barbara Ker Wilson,*
*illustrated by Lucienne Fontannaz*
[0 207 13848 6, Angus & Robertson, £3.95. Ages 6 to 10.]
Blue willow china is very common. Here we are told the story behind the picture on the plates, a design which first appeared in the West in the eighteenth century as part of a craze for all things Chinese.

Unlike Chinese artists, Japanese picture-book makers are substantially represented in Western publishing for children.

☐ 75. The White Crane *illustrated by Junko Morimoto*
[0 00 184311 7, Collins, £4.95. Ages 7 to 11.]
In *The White Crane* mortals benefit from a magic spell but are driven to meddle, thereby ending their good luck. *The Shoemaker and the Elves* (entry 121) has a similar plot but ends happily; *The White Crane* ends in tragedy. Junko Morimoto's *Mouse's Marriage* (Blackie, £5.95; ages 5 to 9) is a comical story about a mouse being introduced to all sorts of unsuitable partners before settling for one of her own kind. The books are well laid out, with clear readable texts and illustrations in a perfect relationship.

☐ 76. Mighty Mountain and the Three Strong Women *retold and illustrated by Irene Hedlund*
[0 590 70498 2, Hippo, £2.25. Ages 6 to 11.]
An hilarious equal-opportunities tale from Japan, in which a Sumo wrestler is coached by little old ladies who hurl him over their shoulders and generally throw him about. Even the Emperor of Japan is amused.

THE AUSTRALIAN DREAMTIME

☐ 77. The Rainbow Serpent *retold and illustrated by Dick Roughsey*
[0 8368 7030 1, Gareth Stevens, £5.95. Ages 7 to 11.]
Also from Gareth Stevens at £5.95: *The Flying Fox Warriors, Gidja the Moon* and *Turramulli the Giant Quinkin* retold and illustrated by Percy Trezise and Dick Roughsey; *Black Duck and Water Rat* retold and illustrated by Percy Trezise and Mary Haginikitas; and *The Peopling of Australia* written and illustrated by Percy Trezise.

The Dreamtime is the mythology of the Australian Aborigine which explains the creation and the early world. The first humans had supernatural powers, but during a period when the earth was shaken by volcanoes and other violent natural forces, the people changed themselves into animals, birds, insects and plants. This is the period that these Dreamtime stories dramatize. Dick Roughsey was an Aboriginal artist who worked in collaboration with Percy Trezise over many years to write down the stories. This set of picture books gives us five tales and one non-fiction book, *The Peopling of Australia*, an outline history drawn from Aboriginal lore and modern anthropology. In all the books the vivid artwork shows the landscape of Cape York in northern Australia, and the huge tribes of people hunting, fighting, magically altering shape, and drawing their history on the walls of caves.

78. Folktales and Fables of the World *edited by Barbara Hayes, illustrated by Robert Ingpen*
[1 85028 034 7, Dragon's World, £14.95. Ages 10 to 14.]
Dreamtime stories can be collected from anthologies of traditional tales. *Folktales and Fables of the World* contains six evocative Aboriginal tales, explaining the making of the sun, the rainbow and fire, the first dingo, and showing the power of the rainmaker. The section of the book devoted to stories from Australasia includes eight stories, each of considerable interest, from the islands of the Pacific. As its title suggests, this book is ambitious in scope, and large in actual volume size. The disadvantage of such a wide-ranging compilation is that it can only skim the surface of each culture's tradition. However, Barbara Hayes has managed to include many of the characters mentioned in this guide, including Beowulf, Finn, Baba Yaga, and Brer Rabbit, along with less familiar stories well worth discovering.

Joanna Troughton has featured several times in this section because she is a prolific illustrator of tales from around the world, and is usually very adept at varying her style in sympathy with the story she has chosen. *What Made Tiddalik Laugh* (Blackie, £6.50) is illustrated in a broad cartoon style, and so it is included, not because it is a subtle interpretation of the Dreamtime but because it is hugely enjoyed by young children, and it does give an opportunity to demonstrate how stories are created out of people's environment. British children, for example, are unlikely to have encountered water shortage as a problem, whereas in Australia drought can be catastrophic. Hence this story of Tiddalik, the giant frog whose thirst is so great that he drinks every drop of water in the world.

## Traditional Fairy Tales

The following stories are among the best known and most frequently produced fairy tales for children. The fairy tale (which doesn't necessarily feature fairies) typically includes a rags-to-riches plot, a pinch of magic, and rules to be followed if the magic is to produce the desired effect; its lasting attraction is created by the theme of wish-fulfilment.

79.  Sleeping Beauty & Other Favourite Fairy Tales
*by Charles Perrault, chosen and translated by Angela Carter,*
*illustrated by Michael Foreman*
[0 575 03194 8, Gollancz, £7.95. Ages 7 to 11.]
Perrault was the writer of the archetypal fairy tale. He worked from traditional source material, but wrote for a sophisticated, literate seventeenth- and eighteenth-century audience. Today's young readers may well criticize Perrault because his heroines are passive and too much emphasis is placed on their good looks. Michael Foreman supports this with the Botticelli beauties that drift vapidly across his illustrations. Even though Perrault may scorn beauty without intelligence (in 'Ricky with the Tuft'), sadly the reverse is not allowed to a princess. (There are now many antidotes on the market: see entry 112.) Angela Carter's translation includes Perrault's morals, which are bracingly rational: 'Greedy, short-sighted, careless, thoughtless, changeable people don't know how to make sensible decisions; and few of us are capable of using well the gifts God gave us anyway.' And ironic: 'If a miller's son can so quickly win the heart of a princess, that is because clothes, bearing and youth speedily inspire affection; and the means to achieve them are not always entirely commendable.' The morals are a reminder that in Perrault's day traditional tales were beginning to be linked with formal education and the sensibilities of the young.

Perrault's texts are long and literary. In the picture-book versions of individual tales, the texts may lose some of their original flavour in abridgement but, if reproduced in full, they take up a lot of space on the picture-book page and are difficult for the young children commonly offered fairy tales to read for themselves.

☐ 80.  Cinderella *retold and illustrated by Paul Galdone*
[0 437 42529 0, World's Work, £4.50. Ages 7 to 11.]
☐ 81.  Cinderella *retold and illustrated by Fiona French*
[0 19 279841 3, Oxford U.P., £5.95. Ages 6 to 10.]
Paul Galdone was a highly experienced and prolific practitioner in the art of illustrating traditional tales. Here he gives a full text, and achieves an organization of word and picture on the page which is well-balanced and will support the young reader. Working in his typical style, he uses the Louis XIV setting.

*Cinderella* is not Fiona French's best picture book, but the brevity of the text combined with pictures from an artist who always produces interesting work is an asset. The story is cut to the basic outline, and a sophisticated atmosphere is created through brilliant colour and a Regency setting.

☐ 82. Puss in Boots *retold and illustrated by Paul Galdone*
[0 437 42525 8, World's Work, £5.50. Ages 6 to 9.]

☐ 83. Puss in Boots *retold and illustrated by Tony Ross*
[0 905478 91 6, Andersen, £5.95; Puffin, £1.50. Ages 6 to 11.]

The plot of 'Puss in Boots' mocks the aristocratic audience Perrault and his co-authors were writing for. A cat can look at a king, dress like a lord, and make a miller a marquis. Galdone turns the story into a jolly romp with a snub-nosed princess and a pantomime cat nonchalantly leaning on the book's cover. Ross builds up the detail of the central character and his actions. Cat whizzes through the pictures, his energy depicted by streaks of colour across the page, and he is still organizing things for his amiable but rather baffled master at the end. Ross's approach will be enjoyed by older children.

☐ 84. Beauty and the Beast *retold and illustrated by Warwick Hutton*
[0 460 06189 5, Dent, £5.50. Ages 7 to 11.]

In telling this story Mme Leprince de Beaumont, by contrast with Perrault, brings out the unusual qualities of her heroine – the stoicism, courage and kindness of Beauty, who in Warwick Hutton's illustrations is dwarfed by a huge palace that has the air of an Eastern seraglio. He captures the steadfastness of Beauty, the mystery of the tale and the sorrow of the spellbound Beast.

85. Popular Folk Tales *by The Brothers Grimm,*
*translated by Brian Alderson, illustrated by Michael Foreman*
[0 575 02446 1, Gollancz, £8.95. Ages 9 to 14.]

Jacob and Wilhelm Grimm are the best-known names out of the nineteenth-century scholars who collected and codified folk tales. Anyone who is interested in their lives and ways of working may consult the essay by Jack Zipes which precedes his translation of the complete works (see below). The brothers were businessmen and academics who collected tales from educated people of their acquaintance and exercised a strong editorial control for moralistic and political reasons. Their great contribution to the study of folklore was the comprehensive scope of their work. They were enormously influential in creating a formal structure for the preservation of traditional tales. They did not, however, call them 'fairy tales', preferring 'children's and household tales'. The English wordplay – Grimm stories being grim to read – has some force. The brothers were consciously didactic, and stories were included as warnings to children. Some incidents are nowadays deemed gratuitously cruel, and so, for example, Perrault's ending to 'Cinderella', in which the Ugly Sisters are forgiven, is virtually always preferred to the Grimms', in which the sisters have their eyes pecked out by birds.

Jack Zipes produced a translation of all the Grimm tales (numbering some hundred) in 1987 (*The Complete Fairy Tales of the Brothers Grimm*, Bantam, £12.95). Most readers will be satisfied with a selection, bearing in mind that only a small proportion of the stories are commonly retold. Brian Alderson's work as a translator is recommended by Zipes, and *Popular Folk Tales* has the advantage of being produced in an attractive edition for the library shelves. Thirty-one of the tales are included, half of which are very well known.

Among numerous other editions, Lilo Fromm, in *Once Upon a Time, There Lived a King . . .* (Dent, £5.95; ages 8 to 12), has illustrated three less well-known tales: 'Iron Hans', 'The Blue Lamp', and 'Six Companions Find Their Fortune'. The book is in large format and has good clear type for the text and full colour illustrations, which show the characters as cheery doll-like figures.

Popular tales from Grimm in picture books:

☐ 86. Hansel and Gretel *retold and illustrated by Paul Galdone*
[0 437 42537 1, World's Work, £4.50. Ages 7 to 12.]
☐ 87. Hansel and Gretel *adapted from the Eleanor Quarrie translation, illustrated by Anthony Browne*
[0 86203 042 0, Julia MacRae, £5.95; Magnet, £1.95. Ages 8 to 13.]
'Hansel and Gretel' immediately brings us up against the problems associated with Grimm. Part of the difficulty is the mistake of associating traditional tales with nursery stories for little children. The wicked stepmother, the abandoning of the children and the cannibalistic witch all arouse criticism as unsuitable themes for young children. Nevertheless, 'Hansel and Gretel' is a popular choice for illustrators and frequently receives new editions; a worthy version of the story must depict the themes of deprivation, fear and the intervention of the supernatural, and guide the reader

towards the reconciliation of the ending.

I expected Paul Galdone's pictures to gloss over the sinister mood of the tale, his usual joviality taking precedence. Although his treatment is typical, with traditionally costumed peasantry, he has absorbed the fearful nature of the story, conveyed gently at beginning and end of the book by a drawing of a doe and a fawn, and through the bleak expression of the father on the first page – one of Galdone's most humane drawings. The word 'stepmother' is not used, but an explanation of her position appears on page two. Galdone has used the complete text, including touches such as the branch banging up against the tree to sound like an axe, and the duck who helps the children over the river.

Hansel finding pebbles in
Anthony Browne's *Hansel and Gretel*

Anthony Browne confronts the issues head on by setting the story in modern dress and placing it in a bleak, deprived contemporary home. Impressive imagery reinforces the parallels: window panes are bars, gaps in the curtains are witch's hats, the witch's broom is next to the ironing board, and a doll lies sprawled face downwards on the floor.

[46]

□ 88. The Fisherman and His Wife *translated by Anthea Bell, illustrated by Alan Marks*
[0 88708 072 3, Picture Book Studio, £6.95. Ages 8 to 11.]
Alan Marks depicts the dramatic events of this tale mainly in blues, greens and greys, suggesting the stormy atmosphere in which the poor fisherman spends his days. He makes much of the greedy wife whose escalating demands of the magic fish end when she asks to be God, and instead finds that all the gifts have disappeared.

□ 89. Mother Holle *translated by Anthea Bell, illustrated by Svend Otto S.*
[0 7207 1814 7, Pelham, £5.95. Ages 6 to 9.]
This is a tale with a motif of a repeated journey. A good sister and a bad sister react in different ways to a series of magic requests and are rewarded accordingly. The picture book complements this story pattern. There is an awe-inspiring mythic quality to Mother Holle, as feathers from her mattress turn into snowfall when she shakes them out. The story lends itself ideally to this illustrator's gift for depicting human adventure against a background of wide sweeping landscapes and clear blue skies.

□ 90. Rumpelstiltskin *retold and illustrated by Paul O. Zelinsky*
[0 948149 47 7, Aurum Press, £6.95. Ages 7 to 11.]
Sumptuous in appearance, Paul Zelinsky's illustrations provide a new perspective on the story, concentrating on the relationship between the king and queen. The miller's daughter who becomes queen is nearly always in the foreground, and we see her change from a dignified girl looking knowingly at her boastful father to a grand and victorious lady. The king, who does not discover Rumpelstiltskin's name in this version (the dwarf is sought out by a faithful serving maid), is shown to be acting out of pure greed. He marries her after she has spun the straw into gold, but he is disquieted by her 'power', and she looks away from him, at us. He is last seen standing behind, and away from, the triumphant queen, baffled certainly, defeated perhaps?

□ 91. Little Red-Cap *illustrated by Lisbeth Zwerger*
[0 907234 48 8, Neugebauer paperback, £3.95. Ages 5 to 9.]
□ 92. Little Red Riding Hood
*retold and illustrated by Trina Schart Hyman*
[0 19 279794 8, Oxford U. P., £4.95; paperback, £2.50. Ages 5 to 9.] 'Little Red Riding Hood' also appears in Perrault with a brisk

warning in the moral that little girls who talk to strangers must expect to be eaten. Red Riding Hood is gobbled up without mercy in Perrault's tale, which probably explains why Grimm, gentler for once, is preferred. Lisbeth Zwerger uses the name 'Little Red-Cap', which enables her to forgo the cloak and make the red bonnet the only flash of colour in the otherwise muted tones of her pictures. The wolf leers, flirts and cavorts in grandmother's clothes.

Trina Schart Hyman's Little Red Riding Hood is a pert little miss. The pictures are pretty but cluttered, and the text is reduced to small dark type. All the objects surrounding Red Riding Hood's life in cottage and forest are shown, whereas Zwerger paints just a few telling details.

☐ 93. Rapunzel *retold by Barbara Rogasky,*
*illustrated by Trina Schart Hyman*
[0 19 279865 0, Oxford U. P., £4.95. Ages 6 to 10.]
Rapunzel is popular with children and well suited to Trina Schart Hyman's romantic style. The dark forest surrounding Rapunzel's tower gives way to a barren wasteland where the purgatory and redemption of Rapunzel and the prince are played out.

☐ 94. The 7 Ravens *translated by Elizabeth D. Crawford,*
*illustrated by Lisbeth Zwerger*
[0 907234 34 8, Picture Book Studio, £5.95; paperback, £3.95. Ages 7 to 10.]
One of the body of stories in which brothers are turned into birds, to be ultimately rescued by their faithful sister. When the girl goes in search of them, she meets the sun and stars, here shown as odd goblin-like creatures.

☐ 95. The Twelve Dancing Princesses *illustrated by Errol Le Cain*
[0 14 050322 6, Puffin, £2.25. Ages 6 to 10.]
Errol Le Cain depicts a classic fairy-tale world of exquisite princesses and bewigged lords in rococo surroundings. He makes the most of the splendid castle and gold and diamond forests described in the story, and contrasts with it the poor patched soldier teasing the merrymakers in his invisible cloak.

☐ 96. Snow White in New York *told and illustrated by Fiona French*
[0 19 279808 1, Oxford U. P., £5.95; paperback, £2.95. Ages 7 to 13.]
'Snow White' modernized in a jazz-age setting: 'All the papers said

that Snow White's stepmother was the classiest dame in New York.' The seven dwarfs are jazzmen, the prince a newspaper reporter. Secondary school students enjoy this send-up, with its sophisticated illustrations, worlds away from Walt Disney.

□ 97. The Pied Piper of Hamelin *retold by Sara and Stephen Corrin, illustrated by Errol Le Cain*
[0 571 13762 8, Faber, £6.95. Ages 7 to 10.]
Included here because the story also appears in Grimm as 'The Rat Catcher', this retelling of a tale immortalized in verse by Robert Browning is notable for its almost documentary tone. The Corrins – well known as storytellers and collectors – effectively convey the full horror of the rat infestation, for which they point to a possible historical basis in an afterword. The illustrations seethe with rats, making your fingers itch as you turn the pages. The piper is a shadowy figure in the ornate interiors and crowded streets, filled with angry citizens, pompous councillors and excited children.

Do also read the Browning poem: narrative verse is an important part of the storytelling tradition.

Another vividly dramatic variant from the Isle of Wight is included by Joseph Jacobs in his *English Fairy Tales* (entry 38).

□ 98. Not all picture-book versions of fairy tales credit the source, giving the origin of the story. One such is *The Man Who Wanted to Live For Ever* retold by Selina Hastings and illustrated by Reg Cartwright (Walker, £6.95; ages 9 to 13), worth remarking for its abrupt, macabre ending.

*Teeny-Tiny and the Witch Woman* retold by Barbara Walker, illustrated by Michael Foreman (Puffin, £2.25; ages 7 to 11) is a Hansel and Gretel type story with tragic overtones. In it three boys, First One, In the Middle, and Teeny-Tiny, disobey and play in the forest where they meet an old witch.

*The Monster and the Tailor* is a graveyard story retold and illustrated by Paul Galdone (World's Work, £4.50; ages 7 to 11). *The Taily-po* is another monster tale treated by him and his daughter, Joanna Galdone (World's Work, £3.50).

*Stone Soup* is attributed to a number of countries. The joke implied in the title is extended by the frantic dressed animals of Tony Ross's illustrations (Andersen, £5.95; Beaver, £2.50).

Each of the picture books in entry 98 reads aloud well to a wide age range.

Title-page illustration for
*Stone Soup* by Tony Ross

99. One Thousand and One Arabian Nights
*retold by Geraldine McCaughrean, illustrated by Stephen Lavis*
[0 19 274530 1, Oxford U. P., £9.95. Ages 10 to adult.]
The folk tales from Arab, Indian and Persian cultures known as *The Thousand and One Nights* first appeared in written form in tenth-century manuscripts but the collection did not reach the West until much later, when it was translated by eighteenth- and nineteenth-century scholars.

A linking narrative – in the form of a fictional storyteller speaking to an audience of listeners with whom we, the readers, can identify – is a useful device for grouping together many disparate stories. In *The Arabian Nights* the linking narrative is the story of Shahrazad, who is given the strongest incentive to practise her skill as a storyteller: her life is forfeit to the Shah's insane jealousy unless she can win his heart as he has unknowingly won hers. Every night she tells him a new story to keep away the executioner's sword, and these include 'Sinbad the Sailor', 'Aladdin', and a host of other romantic, adventurous and cautionary tales. Shahrazad's fate is itself the most dramatic story of them all, and it is a pity when it is excluded from selections made from the huge corpus of tales. Geraldine McCaughrean restores Shahrazad as the heroine in her edition, which skilfully compresses the love story. In just a few paragraphs at the end of each tale she manages to conjure up the spellbinding quality of Shahrazad's storytelling with imagery that gives life to the storyteller herself. 'Aladdin' is retold in full, but for children who want a shorter tale told in pictorial form, there is Errol Le Cain's suitably oriental picture-book version (Puffin, £2.50).

## Literary Fairy Tales

So far, we have been dealing with tales from the oral tradition. The focus of attention shifts now to invented fairy tales. I mean those stories in which a writer has taken traditional characters and situations, or the folk-fairy narrative patterns, and created new stories written in a literary prose style.

100. Hans Andersen: His Classic Fairy Tales
*translated by Erik Haugaard, illustrated by Michael Foreman*
[0 575 03558 7, Gollancz (Lynx paperback), £3.95. Ages 7 to 11.]
Penelope Farmer has argued that Hans Andersen was not a fairy-tale writer but rather a writer of fantasy 'because all his stories are so deeply coloured by the curious, obviously unhappy workings of his subconscious mind'.* Fairy tales, in Penelope Farmer's definition, relate to general experience and come from the collective subconscious of the human race, whereas fantasy may use universal symbols but springs from purely private experiences. Some may agree with her opinion of Andersen's work, but his stories are such classic favourites with children that they cannot be omitted from this list.

Haugaard's excellent translation is a selection of eighteen stories, produced by Gollancz as a companion volume to the Grimms' *Popular Folk Tales* (entry 85). An alternative edition is the now rather dated translation by L.W. Kingsland published in the Oxford Illustrated Classics series (Oxford University Press, £8.95), which contains twenty-six stories.

---

*'Jorinda and Joringel and Other Stories' in *Writers, Critics and Children*, edited by Geoff Fox et al, Heinemann, 1976, page 56.

101. The Flying Trunk and Other Stories from Andersen *retold by Naomi Lewis, illustrated by various artists*
[0 86264 147 0, Andersen, £7.95; Beaver, £2.99. Ages 7 to 11.]
Naomi Lewis is a distinguished and sympathetic interpreter of Andersen's work (see also *The Snow Queen*, entry 103). Her introduction to this book sets the scene for each of the thirteen tales, a mixture of favourites and rarely told works. Each is illustrated by a different artist – David McKee, Tony Ross, Ralph Steadman, Jutta Ash and Ruth Brown, among others – and the impact of a story is partly dictated by the individual style of the artist.

Well-loved tales from Andersen in picture-book form are:

□ 102. The Little Match Girl *illustrated by Rachel Isadora*
[0 340 41443 X, Hodder & Stoughton, £6.95. Ages 7 to 11.]
A retelling, with a slightly simplified beginning, of Andersen's sentimental, poignant story, one of the Victorian street-arab genre. The dying child's visions make ideal subjects for illustration. The match girl is one of the imaginative, vulnerable children with whom Rachel Isadora shows a particular sympathy in her books.

□ 103. The Snow Queen *retold by Naomi Lewis, illustrated by Angela Barrett*
[0 7445 0621 2, Walker, £8.95. Ages 7 to 11.]
Andersen's most complex tale is a high fantasy in which Gerda visits many strange lands during her search for Kay, who has been stolen by the Snow Queen. This picture book will attract and engage the full attention of readers, once they have overcome the rather forbidding double-column arrangement of the text. The illustrations are full of arresting images – the magic mirror, the luscious garden, the robbers' castle.

□ 104. The Princess and the Pea *retold by Margaret Greaves, illustrated by Annegert Fuchshuber*
[0 416 54900 4, Methuen, £2.95. Ages 6 to 9.]
A complete contrast to 'The Snow Queen', 'The Princess and the Pea' is one of the most cheerful and shortest of Andersen's tales. Strangely, good picture-book versions are hard to come by. This one shows the cosiness of a very small kingdom where the king answers his own front door. But it is a pity that the text omits the final sentence, translated by Kingsland as 'And that's a true story'.

□ 105. The Emperor's New Clothes *retold by Anthea Bell,*
*illustrated by Dorothée Duntze*
[0 200 72888 1, Abelard/North-South, £7.50. Ages 7 to 11.]
Though this is one of the most popular tales, some illustrators
forget the serious side of the Emperor's foolishness and treat his
downfall simply as a slapstick joke. Dorothée Duntze doesn't make
this mistake. Her proud, withdrawn Emperor is all too conscious of
his dignity. Colour alternates with black and white, making a
comment about colourful lies and simple down-to-earth truth.
Story and illustrations are in harmony here.
  A companion volume is *The Swineherd* retold by Naomi Lewis
(Abelard/North-South, £7.50). The story has always seemed
puzzling and unsatisfactory to me, but Duntze's pictures, all in
colour, clearly establish the contrast between artifice and reality.
The elaborate dresses of the princess and her ladies-in-waiting are
decorated with representations of natural landscapes. The pig yard
is on the edge of a formal garden, separated from the square lawns
by a curved hedge. When the Emperor bursts in on his daughter as
she is kissing the prince-disguised-as-swineherd, the gates are left
open and the pigs escape into the garden. Once out of his disguise,
the prince ruthlessly turns his back on the princess, who prefers a
mechanical toy to a living bird.

□ 106. The Nightingale *translated by Anthea Bell,*
*illustrated by Lisbeth Zwerger*
[0 907234 57 7, Neugebauer, £5.95. Ages 7 to 11.]
Andersen was preoccupied by the recognition of true worth. In
'The Nightingale', as in 'The Swineherd', a toy is preferred to a
living thing. The nightingale, in Lisbeth Zwerger's line and wash
illustrations, is a tiny brown figure almost lost in the stiff Chinese
court, the background of which is sketched in with the lightest of
touches. Zwerger makes it clear that it is the children who know the
difference between the real and the manufactured.

□ 107. The Old House *retold by Anthea Bell,*
*illustrated by Jean Claverie*
[0 200 72853 9, Abelard/North-South, £5.95. Ages 7 to 11.]
The scene has been moved to a skyscraper city skyline with an old
Danish house incongruously perched on a street corner. Inside, the
house has many odd features: pots and chairs have faces, and the
wallpaper flowers are open mouths. The story is not so much a
hymn of nostalgia for old houses, but a cry against isolation voiced

by the tin soldier who has been taken from a lively home and given to the owner of the old house.

Now we turn to other, more recent inventors of fairy tales.

108. The Fairy Stories of Oscar Wilde
*illustrated by Harold Jones*
[0 575 02170 5, Gollancz, £7.95; paperback, £3.50. Ages 7 to 11.]
Wilde has affinities with Andersen in that his writing too was deeply affected by his own psyche. He created parables with the intention of teaching a form of personal morality. The results are moving and sometimes disturbing. There are nine stories in this collection, all originally written for Wilde's two sons. They are witty, complex and tragic. Harold Jones's black and white pictures act as counterpoint to the elaborate prose.

A Puffin edition of the stories is available, titled *The Happy Prince and Other Stories* (£1.99). 'The Happy Prince' and a few more Andersen stories are given not too brutal an editing in the Ladybird Book versions (90p each) that mainly cut out some of the philosophical discussion; the texts are given the usual Ladybird bland pictorial treatment.

☐ 109. Melisande *by E. Nesbit, illustrated by P.J. Lynch*
[0 7445 1105 4, Walker, £8.95. Ages 7 to 11.]
In her fairy stories E. Nesbit juggled with the typical elements of a Perrault story, making teasing references to traditional tales. In 'Melisande', my favourite from her stories, the king and queen decide not to have a christening party because 'some fairy or another is bound to get left out, and you know what that leads to'. Nesbit also plays a mathematical game, as Melisande makes a foolish wish for hair that will grow twice as long every time it is cut, and it takes a prince ('Why not advertise for a competent prince? Offer the usual reward') to put things right eventually. Full-colour illustrations contain all the comedy, and are particularly good at showing Melisande during the episode when she temporarily becomes a giant.

110. Farmer Giles of Ham *by J.R.R. Tolkien,*
*illustrated by Pauline Baynes*
[0 04 823233 5, Unwin Hyman paperback, £1.95. Ages 8 to 12.]
J.R.R. Tolkien's short fantasy stories are light-hearted examples of the art of creating alternative worlds. *Farmer Giles of Ham*, set in an

imaginative rendering of pre-Arthurian England, is a jovial tale of a man with no pretensions to being a hero, and of his encounter with a dragon. *Smith of Wootton Major* (Unwin Hyman, £1.95), another short tale, has touches of Andersen and Wilde in it.

111. Fairy Tales *by Terry Jones, illustrated by Michael Foreman*
[0 907516 03 3, Pavilion/ Michael Joseph, £8.95; Puffin, £4.95. Ages 7 to 10.]
Stories written by a TV star for his daughter – is this a gimmick? No. Terry Jones has original ideas, writing ability and a genuine respect for the patterns of traditional tales. He retunes familiar themes in a delightfully unexpected way. Jack One-Step helps the fairies take collective action against their greedy king. A boy goes out to seek his fortune on a boat that goes nowhere. Birds sing loudly in the morning to waken the beautiful but slightly deaf Princess Sun. The tales are worth the glamorous production they are given.

Not a man to be daunted by the quality of the opposition, Terry Jones's next book was *The Saga of Erik the Viking* (Pavilion/Michael Joseph, £8.95; Puffin, £4.95), a new northern adventure which follows Erik through mighty dramatic episodes to the edge of the world.

112. The Practical Princess and other Liberating Fairy Tales
*by Jay Williams, illustrated by Rick Schreiter*
[0 590 72170 4, Hippo, £1.75. Ages 9 to 13.]
Traditional tales have been discussed and censured ever since the sensibilities of children became a matter of concern to adults. Tales have been bowdlerized or 'improved' by all retellers, including the Brothers Grimm. Late twentieth-century feminists protest about the image of helpless fairy-tale heroines. The accusation of sexism is supported by the tendency to select again and again the same limited range of stories for retelling. As correctives James Riordan collected *The Woman in the Moon* (Hutchinson) and Alison Lurie *Clever Gretchen and Other Folktales* (Heinemann) – both, unfortunately, already out of print! In collections already featured in this bookguide *The Spring of Butterflies* (entry 73) is conspicuous for its strong women characters, and there are also, for example, 'Kate Crackernuts', the heroine of 'The Black Bull of Norroway', 'Molly Whuppie', and 'The Dauntless Girl'. When I have told this last story, girls in the audience have been known to express disapproval when the girl marries the lord, so that he gets the money given to

the girl by his mother's ghost. This is an interesting comment on the history of marital law and custom. (I confess to being pleased when, in Susan Price's *Ghosts at Large* [Puffin, £1.25], the heroine turns the marriage proposal down.) And Naomi Lewis argues that 'The Snow Queen' is 'the only great classic tale in which every positive character is a girl or woman.' (See her preface to entry 103.)

*The Practical Princess and other Liberating Fairy Tales* is not the only recently produced book of feminist folk tales, and it happens to have been written by a man, but there probably isn't another one with such a good title, and the man was a very good writer who includes just the right amount of tongue-in-cheek humour. Most of the six stories are a pastiche of the Quest. Petronella, who should have been Peter, goes off to seek a husband and lights upon Prince Ferdinand, prisoner to a sorcerer. But Ferdinand is insufferable, and at the end Petronella and the sorcerer leave him to it and go off together.

113. Tale of a One-Way Street and Other Stories *by Joan Aiken, illustrated by Jan Pieńkowski*
[0 224 01158 8, Cape, £7.95; Puffin, £2.50. Ages 6 to 9.]
Joan Aiken's inventiveness seems unlimited, and you should go to

From 'Baba Yaga's Daughter' in *The Kingdom under the Sea*

her books whenever you want to inject children with a zest for story which will give them delight in all the tales in this bookguide. In this collection there is one story, 'Clean Sheets', which is about the essence of storymaking: Gus finds a leaf which helps him to remember everything, even if it hasn't happened. The title story invites us to consider the magical possibilities of everyday oddities: when a one-way street direction applies to pedestrians as well as traffic, but young Tom Mann insists on walking the other way, he finds himself in a brightly coloured dream world of pink cats and pea-green postmen. Joan Aiken's three supernatural tales in *Fog Hounds, Wind Cat, Sea Mice* are her contribution to the Flying Carpets series, now in Pan Piper paperback. The series, originally published in hardback by Macmillan, also includes James Riordan's *The Boy Who Turned into a Goat*, well-chosen stories about magical transformations, and Catherine Storr's joke at the expense of traditional plots, *It Shouldn't Happen to a Frog*.

Joan Aiken has also retold traditional tales, all from Eastern Europe, in her popular collection *The Kingdom under the Sea* (Cape, £7.95; Puffin, £2.50; ages 6 to 10). Both books are exquisitely illustrated by Jan Pieńkowski.

Joan Aiken's tales appeal to children around six to nine. Two writers of a previous generation, Eleanor Farjeon and Alison Uttley, also wrote fairy tales for children in this age range. They are charming, whimsical stories set in an imaginary landscape. Farjeon's tales can be found in *The Little Bookroom* (Oxford University Press, £3.95; Puffin, £2.95) and Uttley's in her *Fairy Tales* (Young Puffin, £1.95). The work of both writers is frequently anthologized in other collections.

## Traditional Tales for the Under-Sixes

If traditional tales are not exclusively the staple of the nursery, as folklorists have strongly argued, then it is worth asking which are most suitable for little children. How do children become familiar with traditional characters? Look at Janet and Allan Ahlberg's *Each Peach Pear Plum* and *The Jolly Postman*. These presuppose an acquaintance with the Three Bears, Cinderella and company, and this expectation is not disappointed. Very young children respond immediately to *Each Peach Pear Plum* and later on they relish Allan

Ahlberg's *Ten in a Bed*, in which Dinah Price, lucky in her education, has no difficulty in handling the giant, Jack, Beauty and the witch, all of whom insist on sharing her bedroom. Dinah's predicament may not in reality be shared by large numbers of children, but as a metaphor her situation is enviable. Without encountering traditional tales when very young, how will children pick up the borrowings and allusions that are frequently to be found in their later fiction? (On a slightly different tack, I once had to introduce *Alice's Adventures in Wonderland* to a third-year secondary school class by way of her appearance as a character in an advertisement. We assume that the transmission of our literary heritage is taking place, and so fail to be sure that children meet the stories they should.) Which books, and which stories, then, shall we use to help us introduce children to the rhythms and conventions of traditional tales?

114. Favourite Nursery Tales *selected and illustrated by Tomie dePaola*
[0 416 96330 7, Methuen, £9.95]
115. The Three Bears & 15 Other Stories
*selected and illustrated by Anne Rockwell*
[0 241 89213 9, Hamish Hamilton, £7.95]
Every place where children spend time should have, as part of its basic equipment, a book of nursery rhymes and a book of nursery tales. Here are two excellent nursery-tale collections, well produced with chunky colourful pictures. DePaola's is large format and has big print, ideal for showing to a group, but a child on her own will need a table or the floor in support. Rockwell's is closer to child-sized, square-cut, clearly printed and inviting to handle.

DePaola has thirty tales to Rockwell's sixteen. They agree on eight. 'The Gingerbread Man' ('Johnny-Cake' to dePaola), 'The Little Red Hen', 'The Lion and the Mouse', 'The Three Little Pigs', 'The Three Billy Goats Gruff', 'The Three Bears', 'The Elves and the Shoemaker', and 'Henny-Penny'/ 'Chicken Licken'.

Rockwell includes 'Little Red Riding Hood', 'Lazy Jack', 'Teeny Tiny', 'The Little Porridge Pot', 'The Dog and the Bone' and two less common choices: a short Grimm tale, 'The Water-Nixie', and 'The Star Money'. DePaola has nine Aesop fables, 'The Princess and the Pea' and 'The Emperor's New Clothes' by Andersen, 'Rumpelstiltskin' and 'The Frog Prince' from Grimm (the latter in Wanda Gág's excellent translation) along with some Scandinavian folk tales. He intersperses the stories with extracts from R.L.

From *The Three Bears & 15 Other Stories*
by Anne Rockwell

Stevenson and Edward Lear's 'The Owl and the Pussycat'.
Rockwell includes one story in rhyme: 'The House that Jack Built'.

Many of these stories also appear in recommendable picture books.

☐ 116. Goldilocks and the Three Bears
*retold and illustrated by Bernadette Watts*
[3 85539 010 X, Abelard/North-South paperback, £2.95]
The story dictates precisely what must be illustrated: the chair, the
bowls, the bed, and their relative size and condition before and after
Goldilocks. The illustrator can decide their style, whether they are
armchairs or kitchen chairs, for example, and can also indicate
whether Goldilocks is a little horror or a likeable small girl.
Bernadette Watts is sympathetic to her heroine, and the whole book
is cosy and friendly. The ursine conversation comes printed in
small, medium and large print.

☐ 117. Goldilocks and the Three Bears
*retold and illustrated by James Marshall*
[0 00 191382 4, Collins, £5.95]
'Once there was a little girl called Goldilocks. "What a sweet
child," said someone new in town. "That's what you think," said a

neighbour.' From her red bow to her brown boots, this Goldilocks is a homewrecker. James Marshall keeps all the repetitions essential to the story, and elaborates entertainingly on Goldilocks' journey round the house. The illustrations show her not seeing photographs of the actual inhabitants (which of course children notice) while contorting herself in the Bear family chairs.

□ 118. The Three Little Pigs *illustrated by Erik Blegvad*
[0 00 661966 5, Picture Lions, £1.95]
Blegvad has given the tale an Edwardian setting in which country folk and country pigs are dressed alike. Into this gentle community the wolf blows, nakedly ferocious, except when trying to disguise himself as a gentleman. The third little pig is left looking decidedly self-satisfied in his ugly red-brick cottage, forerunner of creeping suburbia. As for the other pigs, and children's fears: a child in a playgroup storytime once kindly explained to me that if I returned to the front of the book I would find them alive and well again. This is a firm favourite with playgroups and infant school classes.

□ 119. The Gingerbread Man
*retold and illustrated by Nichola Armstrong*
[0 460 06246 8, Dent, £6.95]
The story is an opportunity to paint a background of authentic botanical pictures of flora and fauna, as the gingerbread man evades all pursuers on his way to a rendezvous with a fox.

□ 120. The Little Red Hen: An Old Story
*illustrated by Margot Zemach*
[0 14 050567 9, Puffin, £2.25]
Its very strong rhythm and repetition make this story a winner at preschool storytime. The breeds of the lazy animals who will not help the little red hen vary. Anne Rockwell's extended version (in entry 115) incorporates a villainous fox, but I prefer the heart of the story, the hen's progress from finding the grain of wheat to making the bread or cake, and the 'Not I' refrain of the others.

□ 121. The Shoemaker and the Elves
*retold and illustrated by Cynthia and William Birrer*
[0 590 70433 8, Hippo, £1.75]
A story from Grimm that is undoubtedly appealing to young children. These pictures are photographed from appliqué work; the pages of needlework perfectly complement the story about sewing,

which ends with the elves running off dressed in the clothes sewn for them by the shoemaker's wife.

☐ 122. Teeny Tiny *retold by Jill Bennett, illustrated by Tomie dePaola* [0 19 278205 3, Oxford U.P. £3.95; paperback, £1.95]
A ghost story taken from Joseph Jacobs. The repetition of the title phrase defuses any fear, while letting children pretend they are having a scary time. DePaola draws the spooks, Anne Rockwell (in entry 115) leaves them to the imagination.

From *Teeny Tiny*

'GIVE ME MY BONE!'

Traditional tales in the Ladybird Books series:

The majority of nursery tales, and many other well-known traditional stories, are available in Ladybird editions, sometimes in two or three different series. The texts are serviceable, though likely to be inhibited by an editorial approach that grades language according to reading 'difficulty'. The illustrations are constrained by the format and by an excessive literalness that does not lift the imagination. They are cheap, child-sized, and readily obtainable. Children, of course, have to put up with what adults give them, and an unvarying diet of lookalike books speedily becomes monotonous, not to say formative of a lifelong taste. Given that Ladybirds are inexpensive, there is no excuse for keeping serried ranks of tatty copies from which the spines have peeled, all too often seen in primary school classrooms.

Other traditional tales for young children:

☐ 123. The Troublesome Pig *retold and illustrated by Priscilla Lamont* [0 241 10921 3, Hamish Hamilton, £6.95; Picture Piper, £1.99] An attractive edition of a cumulative tale in which the pig won't ever get over the stile, so the old lady must ask the dog to bite the pig, the stick to beat the dog, the fire to burn the stick, the water to quench the fire, and so on through a long list.

☐ 124. The Fat Cat *translated and illustrated by Jack Kent* [0 14 050089 8, Picture Puffin, £1.95] Another cumulative tale, this one in the spirit of 'The Old Woman who Swallows a Fly'. The fat cat eats

the gruel
and the pot
and the old woman, too,
and Skohottentot
and Skolinkenlot . . .

and more, until he meets the woodcutter, who does what wood-cutters do in such circumstances. Jack Kent does show the woodcutter bandaging up the reduced, bemused cat. Incidentally, this book was one of the most popular in an exhibition of traditional tales taken to secondary schools.

☐ 125. The Great Big Enormous Turnip *story by Alexei Tolstoy, illustrated by Helen Oxenbury*

[0 434 96680 0, Heinemann, £5.95; Picture Lions, £1.95]
Alexei Tolstoy composed this classic of cumulative tales. He intended a moral, for it is mouse-power that eventually uproots the enormous turnip. Children join in heartily.

☐ 126. Flossie and the Fox *by Patricia C. McKissack,*
*illustrated by Rachel Isadora*
[0 670 81477 6, Viking Kestrel, £6.95; Picture Puffin, £2.50]
Written from the author's childhood memories of her grandfather's storytelling, Flossie is like Dinah Price in Allan Ahlberg's *Ten in a Bed* and is close to Catherine Storr's Clever Polly, well able to deflate an animal puffed up by his traditional reputation. 'A little girl like you should be simply terrified of me. Whatever do they teach children these days?' Flossie coolly refuses to believe he is a fox at all.

127. Topsy-Turvy Tales *retold by Leila Berg, illustrated by Gerald Rose*
[0 416 45970 6, Magnet, £1.50]
Eighteen cheerful stories from around the world, written with 'How to Begin' introductory sentences for storytellers, who are also given practical help with a note of advice from the teller, and an indication of length of telling-time.

## Collectors and Retellers

There are plenty of anthologies of traditional tales available, usually arranged thematically or by the story's country of origin. Geographical compilations are a valuable resource for storytellers, but the thematic arrangement seems to have more attraction for children selecting books from the library shelves. The titles also tend to have greater appeal: *A Book of Enchantments and Curses, Tales of Sea and Shore.* Thematic collections offer a fascinating insight into the recurrence of stories and the variety of people's myths.

128. Johnny Reed's Cat and other Northern Tales
*by Kathleen Hersom, illustrated by P.J. Lynch*
[0 7136 2773 5, Black, £4.95. Ages 8 to 11.]
Collections of stories from one area are always intriguing, even as an unusual gazeteer of a region. This is an attractively produced volume from Northumbria and what is now Tyne and Wear: areas which are rich in classic stories such as 'The Laidly Worm', which

coils itself around the heugh under Bamburgh Castle, and where the landscape, with its castles and windswept beaches, makes an effective setting for wonderful tales. Kathleen Hersom's collection was originally compiled for radio, one modern way of keeping alive the tradition of listening to stories.

Every part of the country has its own stories, sometimes published as part of a major series, sometimes privately collected by a local studies society. Schools now often compile their own collections, and there is great potential for children to learn about the transmission of folk tales through retelling the stories and anecdotes they have heard locally.

129. Tales of Sea and Shore *by Juliet Heslewood,*
*illustrated by Karen Berry*
[0 19 278105 7, Oxford U. P., £6.95. Ages 9 to 14.]
130. Earth, Air, Fire, and Water *by Juliet Heslewood, various illustrators*
[0 19 278107 3, Oxford U. P., £8.95. Ages 9 to 14.]
The mystery and danger of the sea are the theme of Juliet Heslewood's first collection, where characters include undersea creatures and mer people. There are tales that explain why the sea is salt and what the waves are whispering as they break upon the shore. However, these are as much human dramas of the people who make their living from the sea. Interesting variants of tales have been gleaned by Juliet Heslewood from a variety of sources, which are listed at the back of the book. The style is reflective and poetic. A couple of perkier stories give light and shade to the overall mood.

The voice in *Earth, Air, Fire and Water* is strongly rhythmic, the stories selected mainly from the mythic strand of traditional tales. Beginning with the Maori creation myth of the separation of Earth and Sky, the stories go on to explain natural phenomena and the shaping of the landscape. The book is divided into the four sections of the title. Full source notes are given.

131. Legends of the Sun and Moon *by Eric and Tessa Hadley,*
*illustrated by Jan Nesbitt*
[0 521 25227 X, Cambridge U. P., £6.95; paperback, £3.50. Ages 8 to 12.]
A colourful book in landscape format, each double-page spread containing a tale of the sun or moon framed by an illustration. The editors supply an afterword that gives factual material about the history of astronomy. Useful project material and a pleasant book

Emblematic drawing for the 'Air' section of
*Earth, Air, Fire, and Water*

to browse through. A companion volume is Rosalind Kerven's
*Legends of the Animal World* (Cambridge U.P., £6.95).

*Heavenly Zoo: Legends and Tales of the Stars* by Alison Lurie
(Cape/Eel Pie, £3.95; ages 8 to 12) is a collection of stories about
different signs of the zodiac, and could be used in conjunction with
the Hadleys' book.

132. A Book of Ogres and Trolls *by Ruth Manning-Sanders, illustrated by Robin Jacques*
[0 416 67230 2, Methuen, £6.95. Ages 7 to 11.]
Ruth Manning-Sanders was still producing books in her long series of collected stories until close to her death in 1988 in her hundredth year. Picking up any of the books, the reader is in touch with a great storyteller whose energy and enthusiasm fills the tales. The earlier books in the series contain afterwords, which make explicit her breadth of knowledge and her eye for the unpredictable. So, in *Ogres and Trolls*, for instance, she starts with a good ogre, just to confound us. The books have a wide appeal, and there is one to attract every interest: *Heroes and Heroines, Enchantments and Curses, Magic Adventures, Magic Horses*, and many more. Ruth Manning-Sanders also wrote beast fables for younger children, which are published in the Methuen Read-Aloud series. Titles include *Tortoise Tales* (Methuen, Read Aloud, £5.95) and *Fox Tales* (Magnet, £1.25).

Many teachers report a falling off of the popularity of her books simply because her style, and the illustrations, now seem a little old-fashioned. The style is too calm and long in the breath in an age that prefers a sharper, shorter measure. Nevertheless, Ruth Manning-Sanders deserves to be honoured as one of a distinguished group of writers who adapted and made easily available the heritage of traditional tales, myths and legends for children.

133. Imagine That!: Fifteen Fantastic Tales *edited by Sara and Stephen Corrin, illustrated by Jill Bennett*
[0 14 032393 7, Puffin, £2.50. Ages 7 to 11.]
The Corrins' collections for different age groups mix folk tales with nursery stories or short stories according to the intended age group. This book is wholly composed of traditional tales, with the exception of one literary tale from E. Nesbit. It is a good collection for browsing, as stories have been picked from other high quality collections all now out of print. The common theme is that beauty is more than skin deep. Foolishness and low resistance to temptation are the main villains. The heroines and heroes, with honours well balanced between the sexes, win through with the help of a quick wit and sometimes a dash of magic.

The Corrins' *Stories for . . . [different ages]* (Faber/Puffin) can be dipped into for traditional tales. The titles of the books are a convenient series heading and a handy selling point. If the subtitle 'and other young readers' is noted, the books should achieve their

properly wide usage. Stephen Corrin often provides the translations of traditional tales, which are concise and simple. This is
helpful when clarity is the priority, and makes the stories available
to a wider audience. For example, I once told his version of 'Johnny
Appleseed' from *Stories for Under Fives* to a mixed audience of
children with severe learning difficulties, and their parents, at a
harvest festival.

134. The Faber Book of Favourite Fairy Tales *compiled by Sara and
Stephen Corrin, illustrated by Juan Wijngaard*
[0 571 14854 9, Faber, £9.95. Ages 7 to 11.]
The Corrins have used their own translations for most of the stories
in this book. Their favourite tales come from Perrault, Grimm,
Andersen, Jacobs, The Arabian Nights ('Aladdin' and 'Ali Baba'),
Ancient Greece ('Midas'), Russia ('Baba Yaga'), and Norway ('East
of the Sun and West of the Moon'). They have opted to reproduce
Sir George Webbe Dasent's translation for the last mentioned story,
which is a superb evocation of a high fantasy and human adventure.
The supernatural adventures are related in conversational tone
which mixes 'Once upon a time' with precise description:

> So one day, 'twas on a Thursday evening late at the fall of the
> year, the weather was so wild and rough outside, and it was so
> cruelly dark, and rain fell and wind blew, till the walls of the
> cottage shook again. There they all sat round the fire busy with
> this thing and that. But just then, all at once something gave
> three taps on the window-pane. Then the father went out to see
> what was the matter; and, when he got out of doors, what should
> he see but a great big White Bear.
> 'Good evening to you!' said the White Bear.

135. The Faber Storybook *edited by Kathleen Lines,
illustrated by Alan Howard*
[0 571 13992 2, Faber, £4.95 paperbound. Ages 6 to 13.]
After a brief introduction, which gives as sound a set of rules for
selecting stories as you are likely to find, the book begins with
animal folk tales suitable for young children. Kathleen Lines's
achievement is to offer lesser known stories in the patterns of
traditional tales which all should know. There is, for example, a
delightful variant on 'The Troublesome Pig' (entry 123) about a
hedgehog who bursts his waistcoat and is trying to get it repaired.
In contrast, the fairy tales and myths are selected from versions

which use grand, archaic language. The actual extracts from the epic works of Greek and Norse myth and Arthurian legend vary in their impact because some are, unfortunately, abruptly curtailed. In general, the book stands out for its breadth of coverage and felicity of choice. There is an excellent arrangement into separate sections, which shows the scope of traditional tales.

*The Faber Book of Magical Tales* edited by Kathleen Lines (Faber, £3.95 paperbound) is an abridged edition of *Tales of Magic and Enchantment*. It is also a miscellany of traditional tales and extracts from longer works.

136. The Blue Fairy Book *by Andrew Lang, edited by Brian Alderson, illustrated by John Lawrence*
[0 14 0350 90 X, Puffin Classics, £2.95. Ages 7 to 11.]
*The Blue Fairy Book* first appeared in 1889 and was immediately popular, making available traditional tales to children for the first time in a long period. Other colour books came out thereafter at frequent intervals, somewhat to the surprise of their author, until there was a series of twelve. These have been available in various editions ever since. The Blue, Red, Green, and Yellow books were well revised by Brian Alderson between 1975 and 1980, and include careful accounts of the editorial work involved, which will be of interest to readers who would like to know about the development of publishing of traditional tales, and attitudes towards them. *The Blue Fairy Book* includes stories from Perrault and other French writers, from Grimm, Asbjörnsen and Moe, and *The Arabian Nights*. British folklore is a minor part of the book, represented only by chapbook versions of the histories of Dick Whittington and Jack the giant-killer and by 'The Red Etin' and 'The Black Bull of Norroway' from Scotland.

In choosing to identify his collections by colour, Lang hit upon a sure-fire selling point. The books are readily picked up by children, who will not be disappointed once they start reading, even if it was the cover that attracted them.

The work of classic fairy-tale illustrators is worth sharing with children for its own beauty, as well as the insights it gives into the development of the fairy-tale image. *A First* and *A Second Treasury of Fairy Tales* (Premier Picturemacs, £3.95 each), each with classic illustrations, edited by Michael Foss, are economy versions, containing a glance at the work of Rackham, Cruikshank, Warwick Goble and Edmund Dulac. Rackham's work is available in his *Fairy*

*Tales from Many Lands* (Heinemann, £7.95). In their *Classic Fairy Tales* (Oxford University Press, o.p.) Iona and Peter Opie include numerous plates and illustrations from old editions. Among the artists represented: Dulac, Crane, Rackham and Doré, plus the illustrators of chapbooks and penny editions. Walter Crane is represented in *Robin Hood and the Men of the Greenwood* (entry 29). I was very sorry not to be able to trace an edition in print of *East of the Sun and West of the Moon*, that most evocative of fairy-tale titles, as illustrated by Kay Nielsen.

137. The Enchanted World *by Amabel Williams-Ellis,*
*illustrated by Moira Kemp*
[0 340 37603 1, Hodder & Stoughton, £9.95. Ages 7 to 12.]
The last book by this collector and a tribute to her, since many of her other books are out of print. It consists of a selection from her editions of traditional tales from all round the world. English, African and Oriental tales are told with equal familiarity. Amabel Williams-Ellis always conveys a sense of how the stories should sound off the page. The lavishly produced hardback with colour or line drawings on every page has been split into two parts for the paperback (Premier Picturemac, £4.95 and £3.95).

138. The Fairy Tale Treasury *selected by Virginia Haviland,*
*illustrated by Raymond Briggs*
[0 241 02207 X, Hamish Hamilton, £9.95; Picture Puffin, £5.99. Ages 5 to 9.]
The illustrator's name appears above the selector's; it certainly was a superb achievement by Raymond Briggs. Every page has drawings in colour and line, which never flag in originality. But we should recognize that it was an equal partnership between Briggs and Virginia Haviland, who brought to the book her long experience of selecting traditional tales. There are thirty-two stories, ranging from nursery tales to Grimm, Andersen, Jacobs, Aesop and Anansi. Treasury is the right word for this book, which can be returned to again and again.

Virginia Haviland's Favourite Fairy Tales Told in . . . series is now out of print. It was valuable both for the world-wide spread of stories and for the approachable format.

139. Storyworld *compiled by Saviour Pirotta, illustrated by Fiona Small*
[0 216 92429 4, Blackie, £7.95. Ages 5 to 8.]
Storytelling as a dramatic form is enjoying a revival in this country

with companies and individuals touring, and festivals being held. The bookguide closes with a new collection compiled by a story-teller from his own repertoire and that of his colleagues. He demonstrates the range of moods the traditional tale can encompass and there is also variety in the voices of the storytellers from whom the tales were collected. With this book as a guide, novice story-tellers should feel quite confident about trying out stories from different parts of the world. The black and white illustrations and large print emphasize the comedy and drama and attract children to read the book for themselves, with just a few difficult words to negotiate.

# Source Books

Some background reading: only *Tree and Leaf* and *Telling the Tale* are in print, but all should be obtainable through libraries.

140. A Dictionary of Fairies *by Katharine Briggs* (Allen Lane, Penguin, o.p.]
141. British Folktales and Legends: A Sampler *by Katharine M. Briggs* (Routledge; Paladin, o.p.)
Dr Briggs was supremely gifted at conveying esoteric information in a readable and entertaining form. Once caught by her explana-tions and the inhabitants of her robust Fairyland, the reader is thoroughly spellbound. *A Dictionary of Fairies* covers the 'whole area of the supernatural which is not claimed by angels, devils or ghosts'. For the *Sampler*, a miniature made from a much larger, four-volume work (*British Folk Tales in the English Language*, Routledge and Kegan Paul), Katharine Briggs selected examples of eighteen types of traditional tales, and introduced each type. Essential and delightful.

142. The Ordinary and the Fabulous *by Elizabeth Cook* (Cambridge University Press, o.p.)
Subtitled 'An Introduction to Myths, Legends and Fairy Tales', this thoroughly considered evaluation of the place of these narratives in the lives of children was first published in 1969, with a second edition in 1976, which includes new work on television and tales. The shortlist of recommended books has dated, and some of Elizabeth Cook's opinions may be disputed; personally I agree with

her criteria for selection. The sharp clarity of her judgements makes this an essential reference work for readers interested in bringing traditional tales to children.

143. The Classic Fairy Tales *edited by Peter and Iona Opie* (Oxford University Press, o.p.)
The texts of twenty-four of the best-known fairy tales are given in their earliest surviving English versions. Each one is prefaced by a background to the tale, and the introduction includes much valuable information about publishing history. Copiously illustrated from the work of famous illustrators and anonymous makers of chapbooks. Originally published in both hard- and paperback; if you are interested in illustration, be sure to ask for the hardback, which includes full colour plates absent in the paperback.

144. Tree and Leaf *by J.R.R. Tolkien*
[0 04 440254 6, Unwin Hyman, £7.95; paperback, £3.95]
The essay 'On Fairy Stories' was first composed as a lecture in honour of Andrew Lang and has been available in printed form since 1947. It combines Tolkien's romanticism with his scholarship. He describes the art of sub-creation, the creation of a secondary world, and while he includes children in the fairy-tale audience, concludes that adults are more in need of the Fantasy, Recovery, Escape and Consolation which fairy stories convey. Illuminating and inspirational. A fairy story by Tolkien, 'Leaf by Niggle', completes the book.

A recent practical guide to storytelling techniques:

145. Telling the Tale: A Storytelling Guide *edited by Liz Weir*
[0 946581 08 8, Library Association/Youth Libraries Group, Pamphlet No. 29, £5.00.]
A collection of six articles, intended for the beginner in storytelling, to encourage good practice and confidence in telling stories in a number of situations: in the classroom, in libraries, to children with special needs, and to non-English speaking audiences. Different techniques are described, showing how to involve audiences in the stories being told. The chapter on traditional storytelling in schools lists a plethora of classroom activities judged necessary to make storytelling pedagogically respectable. While readers should not be persuaded away from the virtues of clarity and simplicity, they will find in this pamphlet useful information about a variety of storytelling approaches.

# Index

This index, compiled by entry number, includes titles, authors, and illustrators (abbreviated 'i.'; author-illustrator, 'a-i.') of the bookguide's main entries. Bracketed index entries refer to books mentioned within annotations.